Papatango Theatre Company

**THE WORLD PREMIERE C
2023 PAPATANGO NEW WRITING PRIZE**

Some Demon

by Laura Waldren

Some Demon was first produced by Papatango Theatre Company at Arcola Theatre and Bristol Old Vic from 14 June – 13 July 2024.

Some Demon
by Laura Waldren

Cast
in order of appearance

Zoe	Sirine Saba
Leanne	Amy Beth Hayes
Sam	Hannah Saxby
Nazia	Witney White
Mara	Leah Brotherhead
Mike	Joshua James

Creatives

Director	George Turvey
Set & Costume Designer	Anisha Fields
Lighting Designer	Rajiv Pattani
Sound Designer	Asaf Zohar
Producer	Chris Foxon
Costume Supervisor	Beth Qualter Buncall
Therapeutic Counsellor	Ranjith Devakumar (Ember Therapeutic Counselling)
Medical Consultant	Dr Erika López Moreno
Production Manager	Pete Rickards for eStage
Stage Manager	Iben Bering Sørensen
Assistant Stage Manager	Jamie Craker
Lighting Programmer & Production Electrician	Matthew Carnazza
Costume Assistant	Sophie Andrews

Sirine Saba | Zoe

Theatre includes *A Midsummer Night's Dream, Beauty and the Beast, Midnight's Children, The Tempest, The Winter's Tale, Pericles, A Warwickshire Testimony, Tales from Ovid* and *A Midsummer Night's Dream* (Royal Shakespeare Company); *Word-Play, Goats, The Crossing Plays* and *Fireworks (Al'ab Nariya)* (Royal Court Theatre); *Phaedra, Another World, Nation* and *Sparkleshark* (National Theatre); *Britannicus* (Lyric Theatre, Hammersmith); *Romeo and Juliet, The Winter's Tale, King Lear, Holy Warriors* and *Antony and Cleopatra* (Shakespeare's Globe); *Why It's Kicking Off Everywhere* and *Tales from Ovid* (Young Vic); *The Haystack, Botticelli in the Fire* and *The Intelligent Homosexual's Guide to Capitalism and Socialism With a Key to the Scriptures* (Hampstead Theatre); *Wife* (Kiln Theatre); *The Invisible* (Bush Theatre); *The Winter's Tale, The Taming of the Shrew, Twelfth Night* and *HMS Pinafore* (Regent's Park Open Air Theatre); *Next Fall* (Southwark Playhouse); *The Fear of Breathing* (Finborough Theatre); *Scorched* (Old Vic); *Testing the Echo* (Out of Joint/Tricycle Theatre); *Baghdad Wedding* (Soho Theatre) and *Rodgers and Hammerstein's Cinderella* (Bristol Old Vic).

Film includes *The Black Forest* (nominated for the Michael Powell Award at the Edinburgh International Film Festival); *Maestro; Exhibition* and *Death of the Revolution.*

Television includes *Beyond Paradise; Midsomer Murders; Doctor Who; Holby City; Cleaning Up; Why It's Kicking Off Everywhere; EastEnders; Unforgotten; Silent Witness; Doctors; I am Slave; Footballer's Wives; Prometheus* and *The Bill.*

Sirine has also recorded a large variety of work for BBC Radio Drama, Radio 3 and Audible.

Amy Beth Hayes | Leanne

Theatre includes *Linda* (Royal Court Theatre); *Dangerous Liaisons* (Royal Shakespeare Company); *Jerusalem* (West End); *True Love Lies* (Royal Exchange Theatre, nominated for Best Supporting Actress in the Manchester Evening News Awards) and her own play *Cracked* (Vault Festival; *Evening Standard* pick of the festival).

Film includes *Prisoners of Paradise* and *The Power.*

Television includes *Mr Selfridge; Gandhi; Three Little Birds; Flack; Bridgerton; Action Team; Timewasters; Love, Lies and Records; Agatha Raisin; The Syndicate; Lilyhammer; Shameless; Black Mirror; Misfits; Harry and Paul; Secret Diary of a Call Girl; Doctor Who* and *Sirens.*

Hannah Saxby | Sam

Hannah trained at the Royal Welsh College of Music and Drama, graduating in 2024.

Film includes *The First Two*.

Television includes *Gentleman Jack*; *Holby City*; *Malory Towers* and *Shakespeare and Hathaway*.

Witney White | Nazia

Theatre includes *Wuthering Heights* (National Theatre/Bristol Old Vic); *Light Falls* (Royal Exchange Theatre); *Nof*cksgiven* (Vault Festival); *A Christmas Carol*, *Sylvia* and *A Monster Calls* (Old Vic); *Room* (Theatre Royal, Stratford East/Dundee Rep/Abbey Theatre); *Wonder.land* (National Theatre); *Dusty* (Charing Cross Theatre) and *Loserville* (West End).

Television includes *DI Ray*; *Father Brown*; *Holby City*; *Cleaning Up* and *Doctors*.

Leah Brotherhead | Mara

Theatre includes *Wuthering Heights* (Wise Children/National Theatre/USA Tour); *Gulliver's Travels* (Unicorn Theatre); *Lands* and *The Kitchen Sink* (Bush Theatre); *As You Like It* (The Lamb Players); *The Two Gentlemen of Verona* (Shakespeare's Globe/Liverpool Everyman); *Wolf Hall/Bring Up the Bodies* (Aldwych Theatre/The Winter Gardens, Broadway); *Another Place* (Theatre Royal, Plymouth); *Pride and Prejudice* (Regent's Park Open Air Theatre); *Dr Faustus* (West Yorkshire Playhouse/Glasgow Citizens Theatre) and *People Like Us* (Pleasance Theatre).

Film includes *The Interview* and *Jess/Jim*.

Television includes *Hullraisers*; *Death in Paradise*; *Whitstable Pearl*; *Bridgerton*; *Zomboat*; *White Gold*; *Boy Meets Girl*; *Casualty*; *Drifters*; *Doctors* and *Vera*.

Joshua James | Mike

Theatre includes *Shooting Hedda Gabler* (Rose Theatre); *The Vortex* (Chichester Festival Theatre); *The Glass Menagerie* (Royal Exchange Theatre); *Yellowfin* (Southwark Playhouse); *Wife* (Kiln Theatre); *Lady Windermere's Fan* (Vaudeville Theatre); *Life of Galileo* (Young Vic); *Platonov, The Seagull, Here We Go, Light Shining in Buckinghamshire* and *Treasure Island* (National Theatre); *King Lear* and *The Tempest* (Shakespeare's Globe); *Fathers and Sons* (Donmar Warehouse); *The Ritual Slaughter of Gorge Mastromas, No Quarter* and *Love and Information* (Royal Court Theatre) and *Wolf Hall/Bring Up The Bodies* (Royal Shakespeare Company).

Film includes *Cyrano*; *Darkest Hour* and *Criminal*.

Television includes *The New Look*; *Andor*; *Why Didn't They Ask Evans?*; *The Ipcress File*; *I Hate Suzie*; *Life*; *Industry*; *Black Mirror*; *Absentia*; *McMafia* and *Raised by Wolves*.

Laura Waldren | Playwright

Laura Waldren is a writer and actor from Hull. *Some Demon* is her first full-length play. Her debut screen work, *This Is Hell*, which she co-wrote and starred in, won the Pilot Light TV Festival and screened at the BAFTA and BIFA-qualifying Bolton International Film Festival. She was also the 2023 Writer-in-Residence for Pentabus Theatre. As an actor she recently appeared in the critically acclaimed second series of *I Hate Suzie* and upcoming feature film *The Radleys*, starring Damian Lewis.

George Turvey | Director

George co-founded Papatango in 2007 and became its sole Artistic Director in January 2013. He has been awarded the Genesis Foundation Prize and named in *The Stage* 25 for his work championing new talent.

As a dramaturg, he has led the development of all of Papatango's productions, including the Olivier Award-winning *Old Bridge*. Direction for Papatango includes: *The Watch House* (UK Tour); *Here* (Southwark Playhouse); *The Silence and the Noise* (UK Tour); *Shook* (UK Tour, nominated for 7 OffWestEnd Awards including Best Director and Best Production; also broadcast on Sky Arts); *Hanna* (UK Tour); *The Annihilation of Jessie Leadbeater* (ALRA); *After Independence*, winner of the Alfred Fagon Audience Award (Arcola Theatre/BBC Radio 4); *Leopoldville* (Tristan Bates Theatre) and *Angel* (Pleasance London/ Tristan Bates Theatre).

For screen he has directed *Heathen Land* (Papatango/Birdie Pictures).

George trained as a director on the National Theatre Studio Directors' course and as an actor at the Academy of Live and Recorded Arts. He has appeared on stage and screen throughout the UK and internationally, including the lead roles in the world première of Arthur Miller's *No Villain* (Old Red Lion Theatre/West End) and *Batman Live* World Arena Tour. He is the co-author of *Being a Playwright: A Career Guide for Writers*.

Anisha Fields | Set & Costume Designer

Anisha trained at Bristol Old Vic Theatre School. She was the recipient of the Leverhulme Arts Scholarship and resident at the Royal Shakespeare Company from 2018–19. She was named as one of *The Guardian*'s 12 theatre stars to watch, and was a finalist for Told by an Idiot's Naomi Wilkinson Award 2019.

Theatre includes *English* (Royal Shakespeare Company/Kiln Theatre); *The Limit* (Royal Opera House); *Pandemonium* (Soho Theatre); *Mom, How Did You Meet The Beatles?* (Chichester Festival Theatre); *Squirrel* and *I Wish I Was a Mountain* (Theatre Royal, Bath); *Octopolis* and *Blackout Songs* (Hampstead Theatre); *Kes* (Bolton Octagon/Theatre By the Lake); *The Walworth Farce* and *Yellowfin* (Southwark Playhouse); *Alice in Wonderland* (Mercury Theatre, Colchester); *RSC First Encounters: The Merchant of Venice* (UK Tour); *Who's Afraid of Virginia Woolf?* (Salisbury Playhouse/Bristol Tobacco Factory) and *Beautiful Thing, A View from the Bridge* and *Macbeth* (Bristol Tobacco Factory). Theatre as associate designer includes *Camp Siegfried* (Old Vic) and *Everybody's Talking About Jamie* (Sheffield Theatres/UK Tour).

Rajiv Pattani | Lighting Designer

Rajiv trained at LAMDA.

Theatre includes *Test Match, The Maladies, Yellowman, Statements After an Arrest Under the Immorality Act* and *OUTSIDE* (Orange Tree Theatre); *Count Me In* (Leeds Playhouse); *10 Nights* (Omnibus/UK Tour); *Bonfire* (Derby Theatre/Sheffield Theatres); *High Times and Dirty Monsters* (20 Stories High/Graeae/Liverpool Everyman/LEEDS 2023/UK Tour); *Strategic Love Play* (Paines Plough Roundabout/UK Tour); *Zoe's Peculiar Journey Through Time* (Southbank Centre/UK Tour); *£1 Thursdays* (Finborough Theatre); *The Garden of Words* (Park Theatre); *Sorry, You're Not a Winner* (Paines Plough/UK Tour); *Hairy, Let's Build!* (Polka Theatre); *The Flood* (Queen's Theatre, Hornchurch); *SMOKE* and *Yellowfin* (Southwark Playhouse); *Kabul Goes Pop: Music Television Afghanistan* and *Alice in Wonderland* (Brixton House); *Supernova* (UK Tour); *Wolfie* (Theatre503); *Mog the Forgetful Cat* and *Winners* (Wardrobe Ensemble); *Pilgrims* (Guildhall School of Music and Drama); *Final Farewell* and *Dawaat* (Tara Theatre); *Hunger* (Arcola Theatre); *Dirty Crusty* (Yard Theatre); *Dismantle This Room* (Royal Court Theatre); *Nassim* (Edinburgh Traverse/International Tour) and *Babylon Beyond Borders, Leave Taking* and *Ramona Tells Jim* (Bush Theatre).

Asaf Zohar | Sound Designer

Asaf trained at the Royal College of Music.

Theatre includes *Ballet Shoes* (National Theatre); *Macbeth* (International Tour); *God of Carnage* (Lyric Theatre, Hammersmith); *Here* and *The Silence and the Noise* (Papatango); *Sessions* and *Whitewash* (Soho Theatre); *Peter Pan Reimagined* (Birmingham Rep); *The Shape of Things* and *Disruption* (Park Theatre); *My Mother's Funeral: The Show* (National Tour); *Dennis of Penge* (Guildhall School of Music and Drama/Ovalhouse/Albany Deptford); *Sorry, You're Not A Winner* (Bristol Old Vic/Theatre Royal, Plymouth); *Nanny* (Bristol Old Vic); *Captain Amazing, The Bleeding Tree, The Bit-Players* and *Romeo and Juliet* (Southwark Playhouse); *Waiting for Anya* (Barn Theatre); *Bright Half Life* (King's Head Theatre); *Wild Country* (Camden People's Theatre); *The Goose Who Flew* (Half Moon Theatre) and *The Shadowpunk Revolutions* (Edinburgh Fringe).

Television includes *Reggie Yates: Extreme Russia; Reggie Yates: Race Riots USA; Reggie Yates: Extreme UK; Reggie Yates: Extreme South Africa* and *Dispatches: Taliban Child Fighters*, in addition to in-house work for Virgin Media and various media companies.

His film work has been shown at Cannes, BAFTA, Edinburgh and Encounters festivals.

Chris Foxon | Producer

Chris is Executive Director of Papatango. In 2022 he was named in *The Stage 25*.

Productions for the company include *Old Bridge*, winner of the Olivier Award for Outstanding Achievement in Affiliate Theatre, the Critics' Circle Award for Most Promising Playwright and OffWestEnd Awards for Most Promising Playwright and Best Sound (Bush Theatre); *Some of Us Exist in the Future*, *The Silence and the Noise* and *Ghost Stories from an Old Country* (UK Tour); *Shook* (UK Tour; also broadcast on Sky Arts); *The Funeral Director* (UK Tour); *Hanna* (UK Tour); *Here*, *Trestle*, *Orca* and *Tomcat* (Southwark Playhouse); *After Independence*, winner of the Alfred Fagon Audience Award (Arcola Theatre/BBC Radio 4) and *Coolatully*, *Unscorched*, *Pack* and *Everyday Maps for Everyday Use* (Finborough Theatre).

Chris's other productions include *The Transatlantic Commissions* (Old Vic); *Donkey Heart* (Old Red Lion Theatre/West End); *The Fear of Breathing* (Finborough Theatre/Akasaka Red Theatre, Tokyo); *The Keepers of Infinite Space* (Park Theatre) and *Happy New* (West End).

As a playwright, Chris adapted Robert Westall's novel *The Watch House* for a national tour and publication by Methuen Drama. He is also the co-author of *Being a Playwright: A Career Guide for Writers*.

Chris is also a trustee of November Club, a performing arts charity in his native Northumberland, and has lectured at the universities of Oxford and York and the Royal Central School of Speech and Drama.

Beth Qualter Buncall | Costume Supervisor

Beth trained at London College of Fashion.

Theatre includes *Love Bomb* (National Youth Theatre); *The Wolf, The Duck and The Mouse* (Unicorn Theatre); *Kim's Convenience* (Park Theatre); *When You Pass Over My Tomb* (Arcola Theatre) and *The Hatchling* (Wakefield Festival Theatre).

Film includes *Hostages*; *Mr Loverman*; *Greatest Days*; *London's Forgotten* and *Nostalgia Ranch*.

Television includes *A Thousand Blows*; *Trigger Point*; *Top Boy*; *The Witcher*; *The Great*; *The Enfield Poltergeist*; *The Rings of Power*; *Bridgerton*; *Ten Percent*; *Call the Midwife* and *Lockwood & Co.*

Ranjith Devakumar | Therapeutic Counsellor

Ranjith is a qualified therapeutic counsellor based in East London. He supports clients to navigate personal issues, whether related to anxiety, depression, grief, relationships, stress, trauma or personal growth. His company – Ember Therapeutic Counselling – prioritises genuine acceptance and empathy, to create a safe space where someone's story is heard and honoured. He worked with the company of *Some Demon* to reflect carefully on the subject matter and maintain their wellbeing throughout the production process. Visit @ember.tc on Instagram or www.embertherapy.co.uk for more information.

Pete Rickards | Production Manager

Pete is Director of Production with production management company eStage. His career has seen him undertake numerous production management as well as technical and design roles across multiple disciplines. He has managed productions and touring artists worldwide at venues and festivals such as The Barbican, The Roundhouse, Hackney Empire, Busan International Performing Arts Festival, Birmingham Repertory Theatre, Bristol Old Vic, Schaubühne Berlin, Soho Theatre, Liverpool Everyman, Battersea Arts Centre, Midlands Arts Centre, Birmingham NEC, Nottingham Playhouse and multiple UK/EU/Asian tours.

Iben Bering Sørensen | Stage Manager

Iben trained at Guildhall School of Music and Drama.

Theatre includes *RSC First Encounters: Romeo and Juliet* (RSC/UK Tour); *Desert Poet* (Cockpit Theatre) and *GOOD* (Harold Pinter Theatre).

Jamie Craker | Assistant Stage Manager

Jamie trained at Bristol Old Vic Theatre School.

Theatre includes *Northanger Abbey* (Orange Tree Theatre/Bolton Octagon/Stephen Joseph Theatre/Theatre By The Lake); *The Seven Deaths of Maria Callas, Peter Grimes* and *Iolanthe* (London Coliseum/ English National Opera); *The Taxidermist's Daughter, Assassins* and *Woman In Mind* (Chichester Festival Theatre); *Arms and the Man* and *The False Servant* (Orange Tree Theatre); *The Nativity* (Wintershall) and *Maggie & Ted* (Yvonne Arnaud Theatre).

Matthew Carnazza | Lighting Programmer & Production Electrician

Matthew trained at Rose Bruford College.

Theatre as lighting designer includes *The Light House* (Leeds Playhouse/ UK Tour); *Tomorrow is Already Dead* (Soho Theatre/Hackney Showrooms); *Cinderella* (UK Tour); *The Girl With The Tale* (Dance City); *Dance Nation* (Omnibus Theatre/Rose Bruford South); *122 Love Stories* (Harrogate Theatre); *Against* (ALRA); *The Producers* (Bridewell Theatre); *The Collective* (Dance City/UK Tour); *Vernon God Little* (Stratford Circus); *Our House* (Italia Conti); *Tutu Trouble* (Fairfields Halls) and *JV2* (Sadler's Wells/UK Tour). Theatre as associate lighting designer or programmer includes *Here* (Papatango at Southwark Playhouse); *Old Bridge* (Papatango at Bush Theatre); *Test Match* (Orange Tree Theatre); *You Bury Me* (Bristol Old Vic/Paines Plough); *Nutcracker* (Southbank Centre); *Force of Nature* (International Tour); *The Clothes They Stood Up In* (Nottingham Playhouse); *ALiCE* (JVH.o.m.e/UK Tour); *The Mikado* (UK Tour); *Infinite Ways Home* (UK Tour) and *Roundabout Theatre* (Paines Plough).

Many thanks to the 2023 Papatango New Writing Prize's generous supporters: Amazon Literary Partnership; ATG Productions/Ian McKellen; Backstage Trust; Boris Karloff Charitable Foundation; Cockayne – Grants For The Arts and The London Community Foundation; Foyle Foundation; Golsoncott Foundation; Harold Hyam Wingate Foundation; Katie Bradford Arts Trust and Royal Victoria Hall Foundation.

PAPAtango

'Remarkable unearthers of new talent.' *The Evening Standard*

Papatango is an Olivier Award-winning theatre company. In 2022 our leadership team was named in *The Stage* 25, a select list of theatre-makers shaping the industry's future.

We provide pathways into theatre, especially playwriting, for artists and audiences otherwise without access to professional resources. All our opportunities are free, assessed anonymously, and open to everyone.

Our flagship programme is the Papatango New Writing Prize, the UK's first and still only annual award to guarantee a playwright a full production, publication, royalties and commission. Prize-winners have transferred worldwide, earned many awards and risen to the forefront of theatre.

All entrants receive feedback on their scripts, an unmatched commitment to supporting playwrights. 1,589 entries were received in 2024, meaning the Prize continues to attract more annual submissions than any other UK playwriting award – and yet is unique in giving support to all.

Papatango also run a Resident Playwright scheme, taking an emerging playwright through commissioning, development and production. Our Residents have toured the UK and transitioned to full-time creative careers.

Writers launched by Papatango have won BAFTA, Olivier, Critics' Circle, *The Times* Breakthrough, OffWestEnd, RNT Foundation Playwright and Alfred Fagon Awards and premiered internationally and in the West End.

We use their astonishing success to inspire others that they too can make and enjoy top-class theatre. Our GoWrite programme delivers free playwriting opportunities nationwide. Young people in state schools, SEND centres, pupil referral units or charities for refugees, carers or those with disabilities write plays which are professionally performed and published.

Our Young Playwrights Award and Summer School produce talented young writers on major platforms, with professional collaborations and mentoring. Adults join workshops and courses at a variety of regional venues, culminating in free public performances, and access seed funding to support their own productions. Our digital Creative Resources Hub makes playwriting training and mentoring available to anyone, anywhere.

We thus deliver free face-to-face training for over 3,000 writers, producers and makers each year.

Our motto is simple: all you need is a story.

'Every year Papatango comes up with a bit of a cracker.' *The Guardian*

For up-to-date news and opportunities please visit:

www.facebook.com/pages/PapaTango-Theatre-Company/257825071298

www.twitter.com/PapaTangoTC

www.instagram.com/papatangotc/

www.papatango.co.uk

arcola
theatre

Arcola Theatre was founded by Mehmet Ergen and Leyla Nazli in September 2000. Originally located in a former textile factory on Arcola Street in Dalston, in January 2011 the theatre moved to its current location in a former paint-manufacturing workshop on Ashwin Street. In 2021, we opened an additional outdoor performance space just around the corner from the main building: Arcola Outside.

Arcola Theatre produces daring, high-quality theatre in the heart of East London. We commission and premiere exciting, original works alongside rare gems of world drama and bold new productions of classics. We work with creatives from across the globe, acting as a platform for emerging artists, providing them space to grow and explore, and similarly as a refuge for established artists refining their craft. Our socially engaged, international programme champions diversity, challenges the status quo, and stages trailblazing productions for everyone. Ticket prices are some of the most affordable in London, and we offer concessions for under 26s, senior citizens, those on disability benefits and unemployment benefits, as well as industry union members. We produce the yearly Grimeborn Opera Festival, hosting dozens of new and classical works from across the globe.

As part of our commitment to supporting the diversity of the theatre ecosystem, every year, we offer 26 weeks of free rehearsal space to culturally diverse and refugee artists; and our Participation department creates thousands of creative opportunities for the people of Hackney and beyond. Our pioneering environmental initiatives are award-winning and aim to make Arcola the world's first carbon-neutral theatre.

Arcola has won awards including the UK Theatre Award for Promotion of Diversity, *The Stage* Award for Sustainability and the Peter Brook Empty Space Award.

SOME DEMON

Laura Waldren

Acknowledgements

Some Demon would never have been possible without a lot of people. Thank you to:

George and Chris at Papatango, for all their phenomenal work on the play, for believing in this story and bringing it to life

Sirine, Amy, Hannah, Witney, Leah and Josh, for being the best cast I could ever have hoped for

Anisha, Rajiv, Asaf, Beth, Pete, Lewis, Iben, Jamie, Matthew and Sophie, for all their extraordinary hard work and talent

Ranjith and Erika for their care and expertise

Kate Morley and Cameron Currie for all their brilliant work in getting the play out there

Everyone at the Arcola and Bristol Old Vic

Jess McVay, Emily Carewe & Atri Banerjee, for their friendship and unfailing support in first getting the project off the ground

All the incredible actors involved in workshops and R&Ds during the development process.

And finally, thank you to:

Euan Shanahan, for being my rock

Emily Cramphorn & Sally Mays, for providing light in the darkness

My dad, for trying his best

My mum, for never giving up hope

& everyone who saved my life.

L.W.

Characters

PATIENTS
ZOE, *mid-forties, haunted by the past*
SAM, *eighteen, haunted by the future*
NAZIA, *thirties*
MARA, *thirties*

STAFF
MIKE, *key nurse, forties, wears a watch*
LEANNE, *key nurse, thirties/forties*

Setting

A specialist adult eating-disorder unit.

The main space is the dining-meeting room. Basic, utilitarian – strip lights, wiry dark carpets, functional furniture. The only real touch of character is a mural of a tree covered in dozens of vivid green handprints, which covers one wall and lands us somewhere on the spectrum between a hospital ward and a primary school. A pile of blankets and cushions is heaped in one corner. One exit leads to the toilet. A clock keeps time with all the meetings. There's a plastic jug of plastic flowers on the dining table. There's one window, which is almost always shut.

Some scenes take place in the Treatment Room, in which there is assorted medical paraphernalia and a set of scales.

Note

A dash (–) at the end of a line indicates the point where one character interrupts another.

A slash (/) indicates the point where one character starts speaking over another.

An ellipsis (…) indicates a trailing off or an unfinished thought.

Words in [square brackets] are implied or intended, but not spoken.

'Beat' is short, 'pause' is longer, 'silence' is longer still. Long silences should be long.

Stage directions relating to when the patients sit down or stand up are important indicators of their emotional and mental states and should be observed in performance.

NB Ensure is pronounced EN-sure.

This text went to press before the end of rehearsals and so may differ slightly from the play as performed.

ACT ONE

Preset

The dining-meeting room.

The rising sun pours in through the window, catches motes of dust.

Mild classical music plays from an old CD player.

On the table, the debris of a recently eaten meal.

A sense of peace and domesticity.

And a bowl, overturned in the middle of the floor.

Scene One

ZOE *enters.*

She's carrying a box of cleaning supplies in one hand and a pouch of tobacco in the other.

She drops the box on the floor, chucks the tobacco on the counter, and goes over to the music player. Rifles through the limited CD selection – puts on something loud and driving, like 'Atomic' by Blondie.

She starts throwing stuff away.

Empty bottles of Ensure.

Those little plastic pots of marmalade and jam.

A couple of dippy eggshells.

Maybe bopping to the music slightly as she goes.

When this is done, she goes back over to the box, pulls out cleaning fluid and a cloth rag.

She turns into the room – sees the bowl.

Her face drops.

She comes up to it.

She kicks it away, revealing a sludge of Coco Pops and milk seeping into the carpet.

She stares at it for a moment, seething.

She goes offstage.

The music starts skipping.

After a few moments, ZOE *returns with a dustpan and brush.*

She delivers a swift smack to the CD player, righting it.

She tries to brush the Coco Pops into the dustpan but they're all soggy and stuck to the carpet.

ZOE. Fuck's sake.

She chucks the brush on the floor.

She goes and gets a rubber glove, puts it on, and starts picking off the Coco Pops one by one.

LEANNE *enters. She's carrying a ring binder, a plastic box labelled 'KATIE' and the air of someone overworked and in a hurry. She is mid-conversation with* SAM, *who follows behind.* SAM *is wearing a hospital wristband and pulling a suitcase.*

LEANNE.…get through this quick as we can and get you settled in properly after – (*Sees* ZOE.) you're still here?

ZOE. Did you know about this?

LEANNE. I've got to do / a bag search.

ZOE. This is the second morning in a row.

LEANNE. I've got to do a bag search.

ZOE *looks up, sees* SAM. LEANNE *turns off the music*.

ZOE. In here? Why aren't you doing it in the bedroom?

LEANNE (*putting a cloth on the mess*). Katie hasn't finished packing, looks like a bomb's gone off, clothes and shoes and god-knows-what all over the floor –

ZOE. You can't leave it like that Leanne, it's gonna stain.

LEANNE. It's a dark-blue carpet.

ZOE. Just give me a minute, alright.

LEANNE. I haven't got a minute, it's almost nine.

ZOE. But it's Coco Pops, for fuck's sake.

LEANNE (*warning*). Zoe –

ZOE. It's brown sugary milk. Do you want to stink the place out and fill it with ants?

LEANNE. No but / this isn't a priority right now and I've got a whole induction to get through so can we please just deal with it after the meeting so I can –	ZOE. Then I suggest you let me finish what I'm doing or get the Queen of Darkness in here to clean up her own bloody breakfast because this isn't actually in the remit of –

LEANNE. ALRIGHT ALRIGHT FINE. Just get a shift on please.

LEANNE *strips the 'KATIE' label off the plastic box and replaces it with a new one*.

(*To* SAM.) Sorry about this. It's not usually so chaotic it's just admission and discharge days are always a nightmare, plus we're short-staffed at the minute so it's all a bit – bah! You know.

SAM. Sorry.

LEANNE. Don't apologise, it's not your fault.

SAM. Sorry.

LEANNE (*reacting to something offstage*). Oh for – Nazia!

    LEANNE *marches back to the exit.* SAM *sneaks a curious look at* ZOE.

NAZIA (*from off*). What?

LEANNE. Didn't I just ask you to sit down?

NAZIA (*from off*). I'm sat!

LEANNE. Properly please, right back in the chair with your whole bum on it! (*Returning.*) It's just Sam, right?

SAM. Sorry?

LEANNE. Just Sam, not Samantha or Samira or –

SAM. No, just Sam.

LEANNE (*writing on the new label*). Just… Sam. I used to have an Irish Setter called Sam. Well, Sammy. Bloody lovely he was. Had to have him put down in the end. Right, paperwork!

    She rifles through her folder and thrusts a bit of paper at SAM.

First up's the schedule. Obviously you'll have your individual reviews and therapy and so on with Dr Varma, she'll be your lead psychiatrist, but this is all the group stuff with myself and Mike. Everyone off bed rest has to attend group meetings, that's non-negotiable, so keep a hold of that cos we don't want to be chasing you round the building when you get off constant observation – NAZIA.

NAZIA (*from off*). WHAT.

LEANNE (*to* SAM). Stay where I can see you. (*Exiting.*) You're doing it again!

NAZIA (*from off*). Oh my god, I haven't even moved!

ZOE (*gesturing to* SAM). Leanne…!

But she's gone.

Awkward pause.

ZOE *changes the CD in the music player – puts on 'Road to Nowhere' by Talking Heads.*

You won't try anything will you? While she's…

SAM. Oh, no.

ZOE. Cos you think she's not looking but I swear she's got eyes in the back of her head.

SAM. Ha.

Beat.

ZOE. I'm Zoe by the way.

She goes to shake hands then realises she's still wearing the rubber glove – retracts.

SAM. I'm, er – Sam.

ZOE. Just Sam, right.

Another slightly longer awkward pause.

SAM *fiddles with her hospital wristband.* ZOE *notices.*

So have you / come from

SAM. Good song.

ZOE. Pardon?

SAM. Sorry, just – the song. It's a good song. I mean I like Talking Heads.

Beat.

ZOE. How old are you?

SAM. Eighteen.

ZOE (*impressed*). And you like Talking Heads?

SAM. They're my mum's favourite band so we used to listen to them in the car –

LEANNE (*from off*). Sam can you get your bag ready on the table!

SAM. Er – yeah!

SAM struggles to pick up her suitcase. ZOE watches her for a moment.

ZOE. Do you want / some help?

SAM. It's okay, I've got it.

She continues to struggle.

ZOE. Here, come on.

SAM. Honestly you don't have to –

ZOE. I know I don't.

SAM. But it's really –

ZOE. Fuck *me*, what have you got in here, kettlebells?!

SAM. No –

ZOE. Because that's definitely not allowed.

SAM. It's books.

ZOE. Books? (*Struggling.*) Christ, feels like half a library –

SAM. Sorry, it's – they're for uni, I'm doing Philosophy so there's like a lot of reading and –

ZOE (*heaving it onto the table*). I've got it, I've got it. Well, good you'll have something to do, it can get pretty boring.

SAM. How long have you been in here?

LEANNE (*re-entering*). Sorry about that, getting pulled from absolute pillar to post this morning – oh well done.

ZOE. You're welcome. (*To* SAM.) Longer than her.

LEANNE. What's that?

ZOE. I've been here longer than you haven't I Leanne?

LEANNE. Can you turn this off please?

ZOE. In and out. On and off.

LEANNE. / Zoe… *Zoe*.

ZOE. Like a sort of toxic relationship – *what*?

LEANNE. Can you turn the music off. It's inappropriate.

ZOE. Inappropriate?

LEANNE (*gesturing to* SAM). 'Road to Nowhere'?

ZOE. But she likes Talking Heads!

LEANNE (*skeptical*). Oh she does, does she?

ZOE. She just told me! (*To* SAM.) Go on, what's your favourite song?

SAM. Er…   LEANNE. Zoe.

ZOE. 'Psycho Killer'? 'Burning Down the House'?

LEANNE. I've got to get through this.

ZOE. That's Daniel Bedingfield.

LEANNE. I've got to get through the *induction*.

ZOE. *Fine*, fine…

> *With a conspiratorial eye-roll to* SAM, ZOE *turns off the music and resumes cleaning.*

LEANNE (*to* SAM). First things first, any sharp objects? Tweezers razors penknives et cetera.

SAM. There's a razor in the wash bag.

LEANNE. Now I will have to keep that locked. Do you need me to explain why or –

SAM. No, I know why.

LEANNE. Great. Any food, drink or chewing gum?

SAM. No.

LEANNE. Any liquid receptacles such as water bottles or hot-water bottles?

SAM. No.

LEANNE. Any cords, belts or plastic bags?

SAM. No.

LEANNE. And what are these?

SAM. Just calcium tablets. My mum made me pack them. She's worried about my bones.

LEANNE. Right. I will have to run these past Dr Varma in case they're not actually –

SAM. They genuinely are.

LEANNE. I'm not accusing you of lying, it's just the policy.

SAM. No I know, I did tell her that, but…

LEANNE *takes a stuffed animal, unzips it and starts rooting around inside*. SAM *turns away, suddenly tearful*.

LEANNE. I am also going to have to take your phone. You can use it for an hour in the evenings once it's been PAT-tested but only for texts, no internet or phone calls. If you need to ring someone you can schedule a slot on the communal phone.

ZOE *notices* SAM *is crying*.

I know that might seem strict but otherwise people spend all day talking to parents and partners and / so on

ZOE. Leanne.

LEANNE. And it starts to interfere with –

ZOE. *Leanne*.

LEANNE *looks up*.

LEANNE. Oh.

Sam? Do you need a tissue?

SAM. No I'm – sorry.

LEANNE. Don't be sorry, I know it's tough. Is this your first time?

SAM. I was in a children's unit last year, but... it's different, isn't it.

LEANNE. I used to work in a children's unit. It's really not that different.

SAM. I just never thought I'd end up...

LEANNE. Yeah. Well, play your cards right and you'll never have to again.

The clock ticks loudly. LEANNE *looks at it.*

Sam I'm really sorry to chivvy this along but –

SAM. It's fine. I'm fine.

LEANNE. Are you sure?

SAM. Yeah. Sorry.

LEANNE (*calls offstage*). Right Nazia, in please, it's almost nine!

LEANNE *clears* SAM*'s stuff away.* ZOE *discreetly hands* SAM *a tissue, gives her a pat on the arm.*

SAM. Thanks.

ZOE. No problem.

LEANNE. NAZIA!

ZOE (*jumping*). Jesus.

NAZIA (*from off*). Alright, alright, I'm coming...! Keep your hair on...

NAZIA *enters.*

What the hell is Katie doing? Have you seen what she's wearing?

LEANNE. Is she out of the bedroom?

NAZIA. She's running round reception covered in glitter with a great big pair of wings on. She looks insane.

ZOE. Nazia this is / Sam

NAZIA (*crossing the room*). Didn't even get chance to brush my teeth you know, she's been hogging the shower all morning.

ZOE. Wait don't –

NAZIA *steps straight in the puddle of milk and cleaning fluid*.

NAZIA. Aw, what the fuck!

ZOE. Great.

NAZIA. What the fuck is this?!

LEANNE. Language.

ZOE. It's Mara's breakfast.

NAZIA. Gross! It's all over my fucking sock!

LEANNE. What did I just say?

NAZIA. Well look!

ZOE. Don't antagonise her okay, she's having a stressful morning.

LEANNE (*irritated*). Yes thank you.

NAZIA (*taking her sock off*). This is *disgusting*. These are proper thermal slipper socks and everything.

LEANNE (*to* SAM, *brandishing a cushion*). Can you sit on this for me please.

SAM. Why?

LEANNE. Because you need something to cushion your bum.

SAM. I'm alright.

LEANNE. I have to insist / I'm afraid

NAZIA (*re:* ZOE*'s cleaning fluid*). What's that you've been putting on there, is that bleach?

ZOE. Of course it's not *bleach*.

NAZIA. Are you sure?

ZOE. We're not allowed tweezers, do you think they're gonna leave bottles of bleach lying around?

LEANNE. Guys can you come and sit down?

NAZIA. Well is it gonna burn my foot? I've got sensitive skin!

NAZIA heads for the exit.

LEANNE. Whoa whoa, where do you think you're going?

NAZIA. I need to get a new sock!

LEANNE. There's no time for that, we're about to start.

NAZIA. Do you expect me to keep this on all morning? What if I get trench foot?

LEANNE. You won't get trench foot for god's sake, sit down.

NAZIA. *She's* not sat down!

LEANNE. Zoe you sit down as well!

ZOE. I'm cleaning this!

LEANNE (*to* SAM). See what I mean? Just like a children's unit!

Suddenly, MARA storms into the room, followed by MIKE. She seems to bring with her an entirely new atmosphere.

MIKE. Let's take seats please.

Everyone immediately comes and sits down. MARA stares at the floor and compulsively jiggles one leg. She's clearly been crying.

The group waits in silence while MIKE watches the clock. SAM doesn't really know what's going on.

LEANNE leans over and puts her hand on MARA's knee. With great difficulty, she stops jiggling.

Okay, it's nine o'clock. Good morning everyone and welcome to Morning Meeting.

ALL *except* SAM *and* MARA. Good morning.

MIKE. First up, parish notices. Nazia's review has been moved to next Thursday at four –

NAZIA. Oh what!

MIKE. Sorry, there's too much going on this week.

NAZIA. For god's sake…

MIKE. Zoe's on Cleaning Duty until Friday, thank you Zoe. And as you can see we have a new resident joining us today. Everyone please give a very warm welcome to Sam.

ALL *except* MARA. Welcome Sam.

Small smattering of applause round the circle. MARA *doesn't join in.*

MIKE. Does anyone want to explain the Rules of Engagement?

ZOE. I can.

MIKE. Thanks Zoe.

ZOE (*to* SAM). The Rules of Engagement are basically the Ten Commandments for all meals and meetings –

LEANNE. They're not commandments. It's just a code of conduct.

ZOE. Sorry, did you want to explain, or…?

LEANNE (*tightly*). No, you carry on.

ZOE. The rules are as follows: no uncivil language; no talking over people; no talking about weights, calories or numbers; and you need to stay seated and engaged at all times, so no closing your eyes or looking at the floor or sticking your fingers in your ears. And no leaving the room. Even if it gets awkward. Which it often does.

LEANNE. And?

ZOE. Oh yeah. 'Always be honest.'

LEANNE. Because –

ALL *except* SAM *and* MARA. 'We can't support you if you're not honest.'

MIKE. Lovely. Helpful Thoughts – Sam you're off the hook as it's your first day but we'll expect one tomorrow.

LEANNE. I'll help you.

MIKE. Nazia to start and we'll go counterclockwise.

NAZIA. Yesterday I found it helpful having a phone call with Étienne because it was nice to talk to him.

LEANNE. Yesterday I observed the residents playing a board game with Katie for her last night and I thought the way they tried to come together as a group was really helpful.

ZOE. Yesterday I found my review helpful because I got all my requests approved and it made me feel really positive about the future.

MIKE. Yesterday I also thought Zoe's review was very helpful and the way she handled herself was a real testament to the progress she's made so far.

MARA (*mumbling*). Yesterday I found it helpful going for / a walk

MIKE. Can you speak up a bit?

MARA. Yesterday I found it helpful going for a walk in the garden after –

MIKE. Sorry – Mara, can we try to think of a Helpful Thought that doesn't involve standing up or pacing around?

MARA. Fine. Yesterday I found it helpful screaming into a pillow after my key-nurse session with Mike because it helped me release my anger.

Pause.

LEANNE. I'm not sure that thought was very helpful either really.

MARA. Yesterday I found it helpful talking to Katie.

MIKE. Because?

Silence.

...Okay. Any thoughts, questions, observations for today?

ZOE. Just to say, I know it can be hard when people leave and we'll miss them and everything, but we have got someone new in. So let's not make it too, you know... tense.

MIKE. Good point. Thank you.

LEANNE. And to remind you all Katie's leaving ceremony will be just after lunch so if you finish early, Zoe.

ZOE. Yes.

LEANNE. Make sure you're back in here for half past.

ZOE (*to* MIKE). What's her discharge theme again?

MIKE. It's 'transformation'.

ZOE. Right. Classic.

NAZIA. Hang on, is that why she's dressed up like a fairy or whatever she's meant to be?

MIKE. She's a butterfly.

NAZIA. Christ. Just so you're aware, I will not be doing that when I leave.

ZOE. You don't have to do the dressing-up, that's not part of it.

NAZIA. I should bloody hope not, we're not six.

MARA. It's for her daughter.

NAZIA. What?

MARA. It's for her daughter, who is six, so she's not scared when she comes to pick her mum up from the mental hospital.

Awkward pause.

NAZIA.…Fair enough.

MIKE. Anything else?

Right, it's nine-oh-five, have a safe day everyone, meeting adjourned.

As if on cue, LEANNE*'s phone rings.*

They all stand.

ZOE *disposes of the cloth rag she's been using to clean the Coco Pops, then exits.*

NAZIA *makes a beeline for the stairs.*

LEANNE (*into phone*). Hello? (*To* NAZIA.) Straight back down again please!

NAZIA. Yeah, yeah…!

MIKE *comes up to* SAM. MARA *lingers, waiting for him.*

MIKE. Hi Sam, how you doing? I'm Mike, the other key nurse.

SAM. Hi.

MIKE. Sorry, I realise that was a bit of a baptism of fire (!).

MARA. Mike.

LEANNE (*into phone*). Will do.

MIKE (*to* SAM). You finding it all okay so far? Not too overwhelming? I know it's a lot to take in but –

MARA. Mike I need the toilet.   LEANNE. Mike can you do her obs for me?

MIKE. What?

MARA. I need the toilet.

LEANNE. Obs.

MIKE. Er – yes. (*To* MARA.) One minute.

MARA *sighs, waits by the door, jiggling one leg.*

LEANNE *starts rifling through her folder, looking for forms.*

LEANNE. Right Sam, the dietician's gonna take you through your meal plan now but essentially, anything you don't manage in food you'll have chance to make up as a liquid supplement, Ensure, you've had that before?

SAM. I've had Fortisip?

LEANNE. Same thing, different brand.

MIKE. Ensure tastes a bit nicer apparently. Less iron-y. (*To* LEANNE.) Temp's thirty-five-point-six.

LEANNE. Oof.

MIKE (*to* SAM). Have you got a jumper?

SAM. I don't / need one

LEANNE. I'll get her one. Are you a tea addict?

SAM. Sorry?

LEANNE. Do you drink a lot of tea. Or coffee.

SAM. A bit of coffee, yeah.

LEANNE. I'm afraid you'll have to be decaf for now but we'll reassess in your review. You're not a smoker are you?

SAM. No.

LEANNE. Any allergies?

SAM. No.

LEANNE. Any food dislikes? You're allowed two. Genuine ones.

She looks up at her.

(*Dry.*) Don't try and tell me you don't like chocolate and butter, I wasn't born yesterday.

SAM. Aubergine.

LEANNE. Interesting. Don't think we've had that one before.

MIKE. I'm with you there, Sam. Too slimy.

LEANNE. And how are your – (*Quieter, glancing at* MARA.) periods?

Sorry to – it is on the form. Do you remember when you last…?

SAM. A while ago.

LEANNE. A while as in a few months or / a few

SAM. A few years.

LEANNE. Okay. They might want to order a DEXA scan.

SAM. What's that?

LEANNE. Bone density, check for osteoporosis. You do know those calcium tablets won't help you. There's only one way to fix that.

MIKE. Pulse is sixty-seven. Blood pressure's ninety-two over fifty-six.

LEANNE. Great.

MARA. Mike.

MIKE. Yes, coming. (*To* SAM.) Don't stand up too fast.

He leaves for the toilet with MARA.

LEANNE *snaps her folder shut.*

LEANNE. Finito! Right, we'll go and unpack your stuff and then I'll need to get you weighed before we / see the

SAM. Sorry, um – when can I talk to my mum? Just I said I'd call her later.

LEANNE. I'll book you on the rota tonight. Oh, that reminds me, I need to know if we've got permission to share details about your treatment with your family.

SAM. What do you mean?

LEANNE. Now you're eighteen we can't tell them anything without your consent.

Beat.

We don't have to give them all the whole shebang but I need to know if we can contact them about family therapy and / so on

SAM. I won't be having that.

LEANNE. It is one of the most important parts of the programme so we'd really encourage you to –

SAM. It's too far for my mum to come. She can't afford the trains.

LEANNE. I see. And Dad?

SAM. He – no.

SAM is anxiously pulling and twisting her hospital wristband.

LEANNE. Here, let me.

She comes over to remove it. SAM stares at it, distracted.

Did you have to stay there long?

Sam.

SAM. Sorry?

LEANNE. Did you have to stay there long? At the hospital.

SAM. Just a few weeks, while we were waiting for a transfer.

LEANNE. Horrible aren't they? General wards. At least you're in the right place now.

SAM. Wait actually, can I keep it? As a – a reminder.

LEANNE. A reminder?

SAM. Of what not to go back to. I think it'll help.

LEANNE hesitates for a beat, then hands it back.

Scene Two

A few days later.

A fan whirrs on the counter.

NAZIA *paces up and down, 'cleaning'. She is mid-rant to* ZOE, *who is tilted back on her chair with a crossword book.* ZOE *keeps glancing over at* SAM, *who is sat slightly apart from them, reading.* SAM *is now wearing a large jumper.*

NAZIA. It's the fucking manipulation of it all. It's the way they take what you say and twist it and turn it against you. All lined up in front of you like you're on tribunal or in some kind of police interrogation or something, accusing you of doing things before you've even fucking done them! Or not even accusing you of *doing* things but accusing you of *thinking* about doing things, of, of *thoughtcrime* –

ZOE. Mmm.

NAZIA. And all I wanted was a few hours of unsupervised leave, right, not even to go very far, just down the road, and I swear Dr Murphy was fine with it but then *Mike* chimes in with his stupid *manner* he has like, oooh I do wonder if it would be better to take the wheelchair Nazia and I'm like, why the hell would I need to go in the wheelchair and he's like, don't take this the wrong way, *don't take this the wrong way* he says, but I am a bit concerned you're 'looking for an excuse to raise your activity levels'. I mean!!

ZOE *looks up – watches her pace.*

ZOE....Right.

NAZIA. He's not even my key nurse for fuck's sake, why's he piping up in my review?

ZOE. Leanne's not my key nurse and she's always piping up in mine.

NAZIA. At least she's straightforward. She'll just tell you off. With Mike it's his whole nicey-nicey shtick he does, it drives me insane.

ZOE. Oh give over. He's not that bad.

NAZIA. You would say that. He lets you get away with murder.

ZOE. What? I don't do any / 'murder'

NAZIA. It's like once they've decided you're mad, right, every single thing you say and do is a product of your madness. Like the other week, we had a whole discussion about me wearing the same jumper too many days in a row. They asked me if I was 'neglecting myself' as a form of 'self-punishment' or some shit. I said it's a jumper, not a pair of bloody – knickers. It's the only one I've got. You can't even *breathe* without them analysing it. Why you sitting like that? Why you doing that with your hands? It's like living in bloody – North Korea.

ZOE. What are you gonna do then?

NAZIA. What?

ZOE. About the wheelchair.

NAZIA. Well I'm not going in it obviously.

ZOE. So don't you think you've proven his point?

NAZIA. Oh great, take his side.

ZOE. I'm not, I'm just saying if you won't go in the wheelchair, isn't there a part of you that does just want the exercise?

SAM *starts jiggling one leg.*

NAZIA. It's not about that.

ZOE. Come on. Be honest.

NAZIA. It's *not*, alright! It's about how it looks.

ZOE. Who cares? No one's gonna know why you're in it.

NAZIA. How it looks to *Éti*. I don't want him thinking I'm on death's door when the whole point of me being here is I'm supposed to be getting better.

ZOE. Éti?

NAZIA. Yes, Éti, Étienne. (*Off* ZOE*'s confusion.*) My fiancé, he literally visits me all the time.

ZOE. Not the tall guy with the glasses?

NAZIA. Yeah, and he's / gonna think

ZOE. I thought that was your dad.

NAZIA. What? Eurgh, why?!

ZOE. He's a bit older, isn't he?

NAZIA. He is not that old, he's just got grey hair!

ZOE. Okay!

NAZIA. It's distinguished!

ZOE. Alright alright I'm sorry! I must have misread the – vibe between you.

NAZIA. What are you on about, what vibe?

LEANNE *enters.* NAZIA *immediately sits down.*

LEANNE. Sam? Leg.

SAM. Sorry.

SAM *stops jiggling her leg.*

LEANNE *looks over at* NAZIA.

LEANNE. You alright there?

NAZIA. Yeah just chilling innit.

LEANNE *looks at* ZOE.

ZOE *crashes her chair back down onto four legs.*

LEANNE *leaves.* NAZIA *immediately stands up again.* ZOE *gives her a look.*

What?

ZOE *gestures at* SAM. NAZIA *dithers for a second, then goes back to cleaning.*

ZOE *returns to her crossword*.

A pause.

ZOE *glances over at* SAM.

ZOE. 'Spiky mammal.' Seven letters.

Pause.

NAZIA. Hedgehog.

ZOE *checks*.

ZOE. No.

Another pause.

(*To* SAM.) Any ideas?

Sam.

SAM. Sorry?

ZOE. 'Spiky mammal', seven letters. Something-something-H-something-D.

SAM. …Echidna.

ZOE. Pardon?

SAM. Echidna? It's um, E-C-H-I-D-N-A. They're like, Australian.

ZOE *checks. It fits*.

ZOE. Bloody hell, how'd you know that?

SAM *shrugs and smiles*. ZOE *writes 'echidna' into her book*.

(*About* SAM*'s book*.) Must be good.

SAM. Sorry?

ZOE. You say sorry a lot.

SAM. Sorry.   ZOE (*catching her out*).
                                        'Sorry.'

ZOE. I said that must be good, you've been glued to it all week.

SAM. Oh. Yeah.

ZOE. What's it about?

SAM. It's a bit complicated.

ZOE *laughs*.

ZOE. Oh, would we not get it?

SAM. I didn't mean it like that. I mean I'm not sure I get it.

ZOE. Try us.

SAM. Really?

ZOE. Yeah, go on. It'll give us something else to talk about for once.

SAM. Okay. Well it's by – (*Mispronounces it*.) Nietzsche.

ZOE. Sorry? Fuck, you've got me doing it now.

SAM. Sor–   ZOE. Don't say it!

SAM. I've never actually heard anyone pronounce it but I think it's Friedrich… Nietzsche, and um… well, he always talks about about how 'God is dead'. So in society, or like Europe, for thousands of years all of our ideas were built on Christianity and the fact we believed in the afterlife, because if you think you're going to go to heaven or hell or whatever that means the things you do in life must have some meaning.

ZOE. Right.

SAM. But he says that's bad because that's like you're afraid of life, like you're so afraid of suffering and pain that you sort of deny reality by always focusing on this other bigger thing. But then because of science we realised we didn't really need religion any more, so that's why 'God is dead' because we don't need him to tell us what to do and what to think. But the problem *then* is if you don't believe in anything then you have nothing to guide you, so everyone feels this 'nihilism' or like – despair – because we all have to accept that there's no real meaning to human life or human suffering and no real hope that anything will ever get any better.

Pause.

ZOE. Does he say anything more uplifting?

SAM. Well I haven't finished it yet –

ZOE. How come you're doing this now anyway? Haven't you taken a year out or something?

SAM. Oh no, I haven't started. This is just my first-term reading list, I don't enrol until the end of September.

ZOE. September?

SAM. Yeah.

ZOE. As in this September?

SAM. Yeah.

ZOE. How's that gonna work?

SAM. What do you mean?

ZOE. How will you enrol if you're in here?

SAM. I won't be in here. I'll be in Hull.

NAZIA (*piping up*). You're going to Hull? No way! I was at Hull!

SAM. Oh really!

ZOE. What?

NAZIA. Years ago now, but yeah!

SAM. Oh sick! What did you do?

NAZIA. Law with Criminology.

SAM. Wow. That's impressive.

NAZIA. I mean I spent most of it getting arseholed to be honest.

ZOE. 'Arseholed'?

SAM. What was it like? Did you enjoy it?

NAZIA. Oh god yeah, best years of my life, before all this started. That's where I met Éti.

ZOE. Mature student was he?

NAZIA. Piss off.

SAM. What's Hull like? I never got to do the open day.

ZOE. I've been. It's nice.

NAZIA. It's a shithole.

ZOE. / What?

SAM (*to* NAZIA). Really? Why?

ZOE. It's not a / shithole.

NAZIA. Just run-down, innit. The old town's not bad though. And the clubs are great. You used to get double shot and mixer for two quid at, what's it – oh god, my memory's terrible –

SAM. The Welly Club?

NAZIA. Yes!

SAM. Yeah, I've read about that!

NAZIA. No way! Is it still there?

SAM. I think so!

ZOE. The Deep's good.

NAZIA (*coming over*). Whereabouts are you living? I can give you some recs, it's all coming back to me.

ZOE. It's an aquarium.

SAM. It's called Taylor's Court?

NAZIA. That's halls right?

SAM. Yeah.

NAZIA. You should definitely go down the avenues then. Larkin's is good. Ooh and PAVE!

SAM. Cool, I will do!

ZOE *slopes off, sullen.*

NAZIA. Oh and get a house round there if you don't want to stay in halls the whole time, trust me. I lived in the town centre my second year and it was bleak as fuck.

SAM. God, is it really that bad?

NAZIA. Yeah but don't worry about that! Uni's not about the place, it's about the people and the parties and the fucking – freedom, you know? Going mental and getting your life started. You'll have a great time. Plus that was fifteen years ago so it might be less of a shithole now.

SAM. I think I'd take the world's biggest shithole over being stuck in here.

NAZIA. Tell me about it.

ZOE. You should probably be careful then.

SAM. What?

NAZIA. What?

Pause.

ZOE. Nothing.

SAM. What do you mean?

ZOE. No, forget it, it / doesn't matter

SAM. What do you mean?

Beat.

ZOE. How long have you been here now? A week?

SAM. Nine days.

ZOE. Okay, so…

SAM.…

ZOE. Well if you're meant to be going at the end of September –

SAM. I'm not meant to be going. I am going.

ZOE. Right then you should probably start, you know… complying.

SAM. 'Complying'?

ZOE. With your – doing what they tell you.

SAM. I am doing what they tell me.

Beat.

ZOE (*wanting to defuse*). Yeah, okay.

SAM. What?

ZOE (*can't help herself*). Well you're not eating anything.

NAZIA. Zoe, come on, that's – she's trying, it's hard.

ZOE. I know it's hard, I'm just saying she should be realistic.

SAM. Realistic?

ZOE. About whether or not they're gonna let you go.

SAM. But I'm voluntary. They can't stop me going if I'm voluntary.

ZOE. No, but.

They can stop you being voluntary, can't they.

SAM. What?

ZOE. They can section you.

NAZIA. Jesus.

ZOE. Do you not know any of this?

NAZIA. They don't just go willy-nilly slapping sections on people, it's not that simple.

ZOE. All they've got to do is get a second opinion and sign a few bits of paper, it really is quite simple. Especially when you're... (*Gestures to* SAM.)

SAM. What?

ZOE. Well...!

NAZIA. Don't listen to her. They're not gonna do that to you.

ZOE. Why not? They're doing it to Mara. She wouldn't comply and now bam, Section Three, they can keep her here six months if they want to.

SAM. Six *months*?

NAZIA. That's different, Mara won't comply with anything, she won't even drink water now for fuck's sake.

SAM. But why?

NAZIA. I don't know, she probably / thinks it's

SAM. Why would they section her if she's already here?

ZOE (*like it's obvious*). So they can tube-feed her.

Beat.

SAM. They told me they couldn't do that here. They told me they couldn't do that in an adult place because of, of – consent.

ZOE. Well exactly, depends whether or not they need your consent.

NAZIA. Zoe give it a rest will you.

ZOE. I don't know why you're getting pissed off with me, she asked for the information.

NAZIA. You're gonna freak her out!

ZOE. *I'm* gonna freak her out? You're the one banging on about tribunals and North Korea!

NAZIA (*to* SAM). Just ignore her, alright. She's chatting shit.

ZOE (*to* SAM). I'm just telling you what they obviously won't, which is that voluntary means voluntary until they decide otherwise. They suck you in. It's like the frog.

NAZIA. What frog?

ZOE. The frog in boiling water, you heat it up bit by bit and it doesn't realise it's getting –

LEANNE *and* MIKE *enter with* MARA.

MIKE. Okay everyone, let's take seats please!

Everyone sits down. Settles. SAM *still silently reeling.*

MIKE *watches the clock.*

MARA *jiggles her leg.* MIKE *reaches across and puts his hand above her knee. She just about stops.*

It's two-thirty. Good afternoon everyone and welcome to Community Meeting.

ALL. Good afternoon.

MIKE. We'll run until three-fifteen. The floor is open for items.

Long, tense silence.

It goes on for as long as we can stand it.

During this, MARA *starts jiggling her leg again. Then* NAZIA *starts doing it, albeit a bit more subtly. Eventually* SAM *also joins in.*

LEANNE. What's going on? Why are we all so quiet?

MIKE. Is this our first Community without Katie? It always seems to take a while to adjust to a change in the group. It's almost like the unit's a kind of boat, and when one person gets out, it destabilises things a bit.

NAZIA *rolls her eyes.*

LEANNE. Speaking of boats, these legs are making me feel seasick. Can we rein it in please.

SAM *and* NAZIA *stop jiggling.* MARA *doesn't.*

Another silence.

MIKE. Come on guys, we can't just sit in silence for / an hour

NAZIA. Cereal.

MIKE. Sorry?

NAZIA. I was just wondering if we could have more cereal.

LEANNE. More cereal?

NAZIA. More *choices*, more choices of cereal.

MIKE (*writing it down*). I see. And why is that important to you?

SAM *starts jiggling her leg*.

NAZIA. I'm sick of having the same three on rotation. Coco Pops Shreddies Bran Flakes Coco Pops Shreddies Bran Flakes Coco Pops / Shreddies Bran Flakes

MIKE. I think we get the point.

NAZIA. Over and over, it's driving me insane.

LEANNE. Can I make an observation? This came up a few months ago and I didn't say anything at the time, but I have noticed that everyone who is off the cereal rota chooses the same thing every day.

ZOE. You mean me.

LEANNE. Not necessarily you.

ZOE. Well I'm the only one with choosing privilege so you must be talking about me.

LEANNE. Okay well I didn't want to single you out but you do seem to pick Bran Flakes every morning. I'm not having a go, I'm just wondering what that's about?

ZOE. I have horrific constipation.

LEANNE. Yes but every morning?

ZOE. Especially in the morning.

LEANNE. I mean does that mean you have to eat Bran Flakes every morning or is there some other reason behind it? Is it a rule you've made / for yourself

ZOE. It's not a 'rule'.

LEANNE. Is it about the routine or the safety, does it give you a sense of control?

ZOE. One minute forty-five seconds.

LEANNE. What?

ZOE. How long we lasted before you brought up the word
'control'.

MIKE. Zoe, come on.

> LEANNE *reaches over and touches* SAM*'s leg as* MIKE
> *reaches over to* MARA*'s. They both stop jiggling.*

> Leanne's right. It's obviously a problem, people being really
> rigid in their menu choices.

NAZIA. But maybe they'd be less rigid if they had more
choices.

MIKE. It's actually the opposite. When we had more options it
caused a huge amount of anxiety, people poring over the list
for hours, obsessing over what to pick. In the end it made
them even more strict in sticking to the same thing.

LEANNE. That's so interesting isn't it? It's as if people think
they want choice, but then they get given it and they don't
know what to do with it. It's overwhelming for them.

> SAM *starts jiggling again.*

NAZIA. So the answer is no choice at all?

LEANNE. You do have some choice, you have three choices.

NAZIA. I don't because I'm on the fucking rota!

LEANNE. Language.

NAZIA. I'm sorry but it's just so boring, especially when we
have to eat ten million grams of it.

> MARA *starts jiggling again.* MIKE *notices this dynamic.*

LEANNE. That's not helpful.

NAZIA. What?

LEANNE. You said a number.

NAZIA. No I didn't.

LEANNE. You said 'ten million'.

NAZIA. That's not a number.

LEANNE. Ten million is not a number?

NAZIA. That's not the real – I can't even say made-up imaginary abstract numbers?

LEANNE. You know / what I mean

NAZIA. I can't say any number, five six seven eight, that's not allowed.

LEANNE. It's not the number itself, it's the *implication* of the number –

MIKE. Sorry – Sam and Mara, I know it's really tough but can we please try and stop it. It's very distracting for everyone else.

Beat. SAM *stops.* MARA *doesn't.*

LEANNE. Sam can you take your hand away from your face? You need to stay engaged in the group.

Pause. SAM *sniffs.*

(*Mouths, to* MIKE.) Is she crying?

NAZIA *and* ZOE *exchange a look.*

MIKE. Whatever's upsetting you, is it something you can talk to us about? Maybe we can offer some support as a community.

SAM *shakes her head.*

No? You don't want any support?

NAZIA (*covert, to* ZOE). Well done.

ZOE. What?

LEANNE. What?

NAZIA. This is why I told you to shut up.

ZOE. I didn't mean to upset her.

MIKE (*to* LEANNE). She's breathing quickly.

NAZIA. Well she's fucking upset isn't she.

LEANNE. What are you talking about? Upset about what?

SAM *abruptly stands up and makes for the door.*

MIKE. Sam wait a second –   LEANNE. Whoa hang on,
                                                        you need to stay –

SAM *collapses.*

MIKE *and* LEANNE *leap out of their chairs and catch her.*

Everyone else stands up.

LEANNE. Bloody hell.

MIKE. Everyone back up please.

LEANNE. Get her down on the floor.

MIKE *lays* SAM *on the floor as* LEANNE *grabs the obs equipment.*

NAZIA. Shit.   ZOE. Oh my god.

MARA *makes a beeline for the door.*

LEANNE. Mara, no, you're on Constant, stay there!

MARA *turns around and stands by the door, jiggling one leg.*

ZOE. Fuck, is she alright?

MIKE. Sam, can you hear me? Zoe back up please.

ZOE. What's going on?

NAZIA. Looks like you've killed her mate.

ZOE. Shut up.

LEANNE *(rushing over).* Out of the way.

MIKE *and* LEANNE *strap on a blood-pressure cuff and attach a heart monitor to* SAM*'s finger.*

SAM *stirs.*

MIKE. Sam? Hey. Can you hear me?

SAM. What's happening?

MIKE. It's okay. Everything's fine, you've just had a fall.

SAM. What are you doing?

    SAM *tries to push herself up.*

MIKE. Stay down please.   LEANNE. Stay there.

MIKE. Tell me how you feel.

SAM. Sick, thirsty –

LEANNE. I'll get her some water.

NAZIA. / Are we needed, or…?

MIKE. Not yet. Check her temperature.

SAM. Need to take this off.

NAZIA. Maybe she / wants some privacy…?

MIKE. Stay down please.   LEANNE. Stay down.

NAZIA. / Okay, fine.

SAM. But I'm too hot, I need to take this off –

LEANNE (*off the thermometer*). Thirty-six-point-one.

MIKE (*to* SAM). Keep it on.

SAM. What?

NAZIA (*to* ZOE). What did you have to say all that for?

LEANNE. Pulse is a hundred / and thirty-four.

SAM. But I'm / too hot

ZOE. / I was only trying to tell her, I didn't think –

MIKE (*to* LEANNE). What? (*To* NAZIA *and* ZOE.) Guys can
    you shut up!

LEANNE. Pulse is a hundred and thirty-four.

MIKE (*calm but firm*). Sam, listen to me, I'm going to ask you
    a lot of questions now and it's extremely important that you're

honest with me. You won't be in any trouble but I need you to tell me the truth, do you understand?

SAM. I – yes –

MIKE. Have you taken any stimulants?

SAM. What?

MIKE. Any stimulants, caffeine, caffeine tablets, amphetamines.

SAM. What?! No!

MIKE. Any diuretics or laxatives?

SAM. No, how / could I have

MIKE. Have you taken any kind of medication whatsoever other than what Dr Varma's prescribed you?

SAM. No.

MIKE. Have you made yourself sick in the last twenty-four hours?

SAM. No I don't do that, I've never done that!

MIKE. At any point during the past week?

SAM. How could I with her standing right outside the door?

LEANNE. Not on my watch but maybe the night staff missed something.

SAM. No.

LEANNE. She could've done it out the window or down the side of the bed.

SAM. No!

LEANNE. In the pillowcase.

SAM. I haven't done anything!

LEANNE. I can search her room.

SAM. I haven't fucking done anything!

SAM *is breathing more evenly now, though still fast.*

MIKE. Alright, breathe. Deep breaths. In, two, three… And out, two, three, four, five…

SAM *follows his rhythm.*

LEANNE.…Heart rate's a one-oh-five…

MIKE *and* SAM *breathe together. In, two, three… and out, two, three, four, five…*

One-oh-one.

In, two, three… and out, two, three, four, five…

…Ninety-four…

In, two, three… and out, two, three, four, five…

BP… ninety over sixty-four.

A pause.

MIKE. Okay.

MIKE *unstraps the blood-pressure cuff.*

LEANNE. Right everyone, let's sit / back down

MIKE. Let's give her a minute. Can you get someone to watch Mara?

LEANNE.…Alright. (*To the other patients.*) Come on guys.

NAZIA *and* MARA *make for the door.* ZOE *lingers, still looking at* SAM, *wracked with guilt.*

Zoe.

ZOE *follows them out.*

MIKE *stands up and puts the obs equipment away.*

SAM *tries to get up.*

MIKE. Stay there please.

SAM.…What happened?

MIKE. Postural hypotension. Also known as standing up too fast when you have dangerously low blood pressure, hence why I told you to be careful. You're lucky it happened here and not getting up from the toilet, or you might have cracked your head open.

SAM. But it's never made my heart go like that, or my breathing.

MIKE. I think that was preceded by a panic attack. Have you ever had one of those before?

I'm sorry to have given you the third degree but we have had people go into seizures and cardiac arrest so we can't afford to take any chances. How do you feel now?

SAM. Tired.

MIKE. Not sick or dizzy?

SAM. No.

MIKE. Too hot still?

SAM. No.

MIKE. Good.

LEANNE *re-enters with water, which she brings to* SAM.

LEANNE. Here, have some water.

She hands it to SAM. SAM *doesn't drink any.*

MIKE. Do you want tell us what that was all about?

Silence.

LEANNE *looks at the clock.*

LEANNE (*to* MIKE). We should really carry on –

SAM. I can't.

LEANNE. We can't just cancel Community, it wouldn't be fair on everyone else.

SAM. Can I go to my room for a bit? Just for a bit.

LEANNE. You're on Constant so I'd have to get someone to go
with you.

SAM. Can't I just stay in the corridor then?

LEANNE. I'm sorry but everyone off bed rest has to attend
group meetings at all times, that's non-negotiable.

MIKE. Sam what's going on?

SAM. Are you gonna stop me going to uni?

LEANNE and MIKE *are taken aback.*

God you are aren't you, I knew I knew I never should have
come here –

MIKE. Whoa, slow down.

LEANNE. When did we ever say we'd stop you going to uni?

SAM. Zoe said you would, she said –

LEANNE. Oh *Zoe* said that did she? (*To* MIKE.) Great.

SAM. Yes she said you –

LEANNE. And is Zoe your key nurse or am I?

SAM. You but –

LEANNE. Is Zoe your psychiatrist or your therapist or your
nutritionist?

SAM. No but she –

LEANNE. So who do you think you should be listening to here,
your care team or one of the other patients?

SAM. What if I said I wanted to leave?

LEANNE. What?

SAM. If I said I wanted to leave, what would happen?

Pause.

MIKE *and* LEANNE *exchange a glance.*

LEANNE. We don't really have time for this / right now

SAM. I'm voluntary. Yes?

LEANNE. Can we talk about this later?

SAM. So if I said I wanted to leave, right now, I could go?

LEANNE. Is that what you're saying?

SAM. I'm saying if I did say that.

LEANNE. But *are* you saying that?

SAM. No I'm not necessarily / saying that but if I did

LEANNE. Then we don't need to get into / it right now

SAM. *If I did* – what would happen?

MIKE. Do you really think that's for the best Sam? Do you think you're well enough to go?

SAM. I know I'm not fine but I'm not as bad as them.

LEANNE. Who? The other patients?

SAM. Yeah.

LEANNE. And you don't think they think that? That they're not as bad as you?

SAM. But I'm actually not, like I'm not as bad as Mara.

LEANNE. Unless I'm seeing things it's you who just collapsed on the floor, not Mara.

SAM. You know what I mean.

LEANNE. No I don't actually.

SAM. I'm not ill in here – (*i.e. in the head.*) like she is. I'm not acting like she is.

LEANNE. And how does that make you feel? Superior or inferior?

Tiny beat.

SAM. What?

LEANNE. Why won't you drink any water?

SAM. Because – what? I don't want any.

LEANNE. That's odd. A minute ago you said you were thirsty.

SAM. That isn't – you're avoiding the question, that isn't relevant.

LEANNE. You're asking us whether we'd recommend your discharge so I'm afraid it is relevant.

SAM. So would you then? Would you recommend it?

LEANNE. If you said that you wanted to leave?

SAM. Yes.

LEANNE. Today?

SAM. Yes.

LEANNE. Who would we be talking to in that scenario, Sam or the eating disorder?

SAM. I – me, Sam!

LEANNE. Are you sure?

SAM. Yes!

LEANNE. Okay well based on what I've seen over the last week I'd have to say no.

SAM. But it's not up to you is it?

LEANNE. No but given you've not put any weight on since / you got here

SAM. I have. I definitely have.

LEANNE. Come on Sam, you know you haven't.

SAM. But it's not just about that –

LEANNE. It is when you're in the state you're in. And that being the case I can't see the psychiatric team thinking it's a good idea.

SAM. So what if I ignored them?

LEANNE. If you discharged yourself against medical advice?

SAM. What would that mean?

LEANNE. Well it's hard to say until we have / that conversation

SAM. What would it mean?

LEANNE. It doesn't really matter unless we got to that point so / if you're not actually

SAM. For fuck's sake can you please just tell me the truth!

LEANNE. I can't say for sure. But I think you'd be putting them in a very difficult position.

SAM *absorbs this – crumples*.

Pause.

Do you want a tissue?

SAM *(tearful)*. No I don't want a – fucking tissue.

LEANNE. Okay, alright.

Pause.

SAM. Please? Please just, please don't take this away from me. You don't understand, I can't... I need this. I need a reason to do it or I'll never be able to... [stop.]

MIKE *and* LEANNE *exchange a look*. MIKE *crouches in front of* SAM.

MIKE *(gentle)*. Sam, listen. This is not a prison. We're not here to punish you or threaten you or lock you up. We want you to get well and go to university and get on with the rest of your life. You know who doesn't want that? Your illness. It wants to keep a hold of you until it kills you, because it'll never be satisfied with anything less.

SAM. I'm not / gonna

MIKE. I know you think that won't happen to you, that's what everyone thinks. And we wouldn't be doing our jobs properly if we took that risk. So if you can trust us, and let us help you over the next few months, then I promise you, the last thing any of us want to do is stop you from going.

Because we're on Sam's side, okay? Not the anorexia's side. Sam's. And we don't want you to end up straight back in hospital again or worse.

LEANNE. You were right before, Sam. Adult units are different. If you don't get out and stay out, it's a bloody long road.

MIKE *offers* SAM *a tissue, which she takes.*

MIKE. So what do you say? Do we have a deal?

Blackout.

Time passes.

In the darkness, a nightmare.

Voices, shouting, escalating to a scream –

Then abruptly –

ACT TWO

Scene One

Lights up.

The Treatment Room, 5:30 a.m.

ZOE *is wearing a hospital gown, sat on a chair, half-asleep.*
MIKE *is taking her bloods.*

The clock ticks loudly.

MIKE. Fist relaxed.

ZOE *relaxes her fist.*

Few moments of silence while the blood fills up the vial.

Then MIKE *pulls the needle out.*

Okay. Done.

He presses a ball of cotton wool into the crook of ZOE*'s
elbow – she replaces his fingers and presses down.
Practised; she's done this a million times.* MIKE *puts the
samples away.*

ZOE. You're much better at that than Leanne.

MIKE. Am I?

ZOE. Mm. Last time she did it I had a bruise the size of
a pancake. I couldn't bend my arm for two days.

MIKE. You have got difficult veins.

MIKE *flips through* ZOE*'s folder, looking for her weight
chart.* ZOE *yawns extravagantly.*

Take it you didn't sleep well.

ZOE. I didn't sleep at all.

MIKE. Yeah, I heard there was a bit of a… disturbance.

ZOE. That's a fucking understatement.

MIKE. That's how it was described in handover.

ZOE. What was she doing? Getting out of bed and doing circuit training?

MIKE. Have you been to the loo?

ZOE. Trying to kill one of the night staff? Yes.

MIKE. Number one or number two?

ZOE. Number one.

MIKE. No fluids since?

ZOE. No. Christ, I've been / awake since two

MIKE. When was the last number two?

ZOE. What?

MIKE. The last number two, when was it?

ZOE. I don't know. Monday, I think.

MIKE. And what was it like?

ZOE. Like shitting iron.

MIKE. Right. I'll talk to Dr Murphy about getting another stool sample.

ZOE. / Great.

MIKE. Because that shouldn't still be the case with all the docusate / you're on

ZOE. Yeah well it's not helping.

MIKE. We are starting to wonder if it isn't more of a psychological… block.

Beat.

How's the reflux? The cough's sounding a lot –

ZOE. Better. Still burning but no more [bile].

ZOE gets on the scale backwards, facing away from the numbers.

MIKE. You got anything fun planned for your leave this weekend?

ZOE. Dunno. Sit in my pants watching *Golden Balls*. Have a wank and a cry and a bottle of wine. The usual.

MIKE. I thought we talked about you getting out the house more.

ZOE. It was a joke.

MIKE. Yes, I know.

The scale beeps.

You can alight.

ZOE gets off. MIKE writes her weight in his chart. ZOE starts getting changed back into her pyjamas and dressing gown.

I'm just saying. It's meant to be good weather. You could go out, do something nice. Or you could apply for that TA course we were talking about, the part-time one. We can look over the forms today if you want.

ZOE says nothing, continues getting dressed.

What?

ZOE. I didn't say anything.

MIKE. Seems like there's something on your mind.

Come on, use your words.

ZOE. It's not –

Beat.

Mara. It's just getting ridiculous now.

MIKE. Look I'm sorry about last night, I'm gonna talk to the
night staff and make sure they know / how to handle her

ZOE. It's not just that. It's all of it. You and Leanne run round
after her like madmen.

MIKE. It's just really difficult with the staffing shortage –

ZOE. The pair of you are in here with her for forty minutes after
every meal.

MIKE. She's… struggling a lot at the minute, so –

ZOE. Well I'm really sorry to hear that Mike but she's not the
only one here.

Beat.

MIKE. Do you feel like you need some extra support after meals?

ZOE. No.

MIKE. You haven't been –

ZOE. No.

MIKE. Or thinking about – ?

ZOE. No.

MIKE. Because you know you should tell us if –

ZOE. Yes.

MIKE. And you've been doing so well this time round in terms
of honesty –

ZOE. Jesus, it's not about that, I'm not even talking about me.

MIKE. Who are you talking about then?

*He realises; sense they've had this conversation several
times before.*

Right. Okay.

ZOE. She's still hardly speaking in groups. That's true, you
can't tell me I'm imagining it.

MIKE. Yes but like I've said, she's eighteen. She's on a ward full of older women.

ZOE. But she's been here what, nine weeks now? Isn't that long enough to stop being intimidated?

MIKE. Some people just don't say that much in the groups, not everyone's as comfortable voicing an opinion as you are. (*Off* ZOE*'s look*.) That sounded – I don't mean it in a bad way. It's a good thing. But it's different strokes for different folks.

ZOE. But I never see her with Leanne any more, she's always off on her own, reading.

MIKE. She's studious isn't she. And it helps having something to focus on, it's motivating, which is why I keep banging on at you about this TA thing –

ZOE. She spends all her time in her room.

MIKE. Again, that's not necessarily sinister –

ZOE. You wouldn't know because you're all too wrapped up in Mara to pay her any attention!

MIKE. Look I know I'm not her key nurse but I still see her every day. She's doing well. Really well, in fact. She's completing her meal plan, she's hitting her targets every week –

ZOE. But that's just surface stuff, that's not –

MIKE. I know that but she's also motivated, she's engaged, she's managing her leave, she's actually doing a lot better than any of us thought she would.

ZOE. But she doesn't talk to anyone.

MIKE. Okay. Do you ever talk to her?

ZOE. I – no.

MIKE. Why not?

ZOE. Because she hates me / and it's not my job to talk to her

MIKE. She doesn't hate you. Why would she hate you? Is this still about the whole sectioning palaver?

ZOE (*yes*). No.

MIKE. Because I know you felt terrible about that but if it was meant to be a wake-up call then it worked. You need to stop torturing yourself.

ZOE *continues getting dressed*.

Look I was gonna wait till your review to bring this up but Gemma called again.

ZOE *goes still*.

ZOE. What did she want.

MIKE. Same as always. Information. About you, and how you are.

ZOE. What did you tell her?

MIKE. Obviously I couldn't tell her anything / as per your wishes

ZOE. Good, keep it that way.

MIKE. But I *would* have said you've made more progress this admission than any other time you've been here. I think she'd like to hear that coming from you. She asked me to give you her number.

ZOE. I don't want it.

MIKE. Don't you think it'd be a good idea to speak to her? You've been doing so well Zoe. I really think it's time we started pushing you a bit. And I've resisted saying this but I worry this whole Sam thing might be you projecting.

ZOE. Projecting?

MIKE. Because of / Mol–

ZOE. It's not about that.

MIKE *senses he shouldn't push this further now*.

MIKE. Just remember you're here for you, okay? Not for Sam or anyone else. You need to focus on yourself.

Scene Two

The dining-meeting room. Evening.

SAM *is sat at the table with a load of art supplies in front of her, drawing something on an A3 piece of paper.*

She does indeed look different than she did in the first act – she's no longer wearing a jumper, and there's a shine or glow to her that wasn't there before.

She leans over to grab a rubber and accidentally knocks her pot of pencils on the floor.

She gets up to sort the mess then abruptly freezes.

A few seconds pass.

She opens her trousers and looks inside her pants.

Her period has come back.

She stands there staring for a long moment.

Then does her trousers back up.

She takes several tissues from the box, folds them up into a makeshift sanitary pad and puts it inside her pants.

She stands in the middle of the room not knowing what to do with herself.

She goes and sits on the chair. She stands up again. She takes the cushion off the chair and throws it to one side. She sits down again. She wriggles around in the chair, feeling for her sit bones.

(She can't feel them.)

She takes the hospital wristband out of her pocket and wraps it around her wrist, then further up her arm.

(It doesn't go very far.)

She crawls out of her skin.

She picks up a pencil, wipes the end off on her T-shirt, goes into the toilet and shuts the door.

We hear the tap go on.

ZOE enters. Again, she is post-cigarette, carrying the box of cleaning products and the pouch of tobacco, which she chucks on the counter.

She catches sight of the drawing on the table. Looks at it.

There's a cough from the toilet offstage.

ZOE *looks up.*

Listens.

The toilet flushes. The tap goes off. ZOE *moves away into the shadows.*

SAM *emerges. She takes a packet of gum from her bra and puts one in her mouth.* ZOE, *by the counter, watches from the corner of her eye.*

As SAM *comes further into the room she notices* ZOE.

SAM. Oh. Hi.

ZOE. Hello.

Beat.

SAM. Do you need to / clean up or

ZOE. I was just / coming to

SAM. I thought Nazia was on duty.

ZOE. She's gone on overnight leave.

Beat.

I'll come back later.

SAM. It's fine. I'm done, so.

SAM *starts packing up her stuff. She surreptitiously wipes the end of the pencil she just took into the toilet on her T-shirt.*

ZOE. That's a cool drawing.

Sorry, it was just there, I didn't mean to pry.

Is that just for fun?

SAM. It's for Leanne.

Beat.

ZOE. You've drawn a picture for Leanne?

SAM. No.

ZOE. That's cute.

SAM (*somewhere between annoyed and amused*). It's not *for her*, it's for my key-nurse session, it's art therapy.

There's some sense this has helped break whatever tension there was.

ZOE. No, I know. I'm sure she'll be very impressed. It's like actual proper art.

Can I have another look?

SAM shrugs. ZOE comes over and looks at the drawing.

SAM hangs back, surreptitiously adjusting her underwear.

What... is it?

SAM. It's a self-portrait.

ZOE. Ah. A classic. So... where are you?

SAM. That's me when I was twelve, before... and that's me now.

ZOE. What's this big mouth screaming in your ear? Is that Leanne?

Beat.

Oh.

SAM. It's supposed to represent the 'voice' or whatever, I don't know.

ZOE. No, that makes sense. That's funny, I've never pictured it like that.

SAM. How do you picture it?

ZOE. Like some big evil demon. Or like God. Or maybe just like me, but… thinner.

SAM shifts, physically uncomfortable.

Who are these people with guns?

SAM. My parents. (*Off* ZOE's *look.*) It's not literal, it's – they're getting a divorce, it's supposed to be them having a fight. I mean they're not violent or anything. My dad did kick a chair across the room in family therapy once, but that's not – it's whatever, it's fine. (*Sensing she has revealed too much.*) He didn't kick it *at me.* I've done worse anyway. I threw a plate of lasagne at his head, like actually at his head.

ZOE.…Right.

SAM. It's just sort of how we were. We all took turns being the monster. Sometimes it was him. Sometimes it was my mum. Most of the time it was me.

ZOE. You? Why you?

SAM. Because… I don't know. They were scared of me I guess? Or of my… the way I am. That's why they're splitting up.

ZOE. But you're just a kid.

This triggers something in SAM. *She's conscious of the blood, and what it means.*

SAM. I'm not a kid though am I?

ZOE. You're eighteen, you're a kid, you can't hold yourself responsible for –

SAM. Anyway whatever, it's just a stupid – I'm getting out of there so it doesn't really matter any more.

SAM packs up her stuff up to leave.

ZOE is at war with herself.

ZOE (*abruptly*). I've got a niece.

SAM turns.

My twin sister Gemma's girl. She's called Molly.

SAM....Okay.

Pause.

I didn't know you had a twin sister.

ZOE. I don't any more.

SAM. She's dead?

ZOE. She's – no, Jesus, she's not dead.

SAM. So what – ?

ZOE. I'm telling you aren't I.

I have a really bad problem with purging. Bingeing and
purging. I go back and forth between that and starvation,
I have done for years, it's like the only way I can kick one of
them is to pick up the other so I'll starve and purge whatever
I do eat until I snap and then I'll binge and purge until I fuck
myself up and that's usually what lands me...

A few years ago me and Gemma had some big argument.
I can't even remember what it was about, but it set me off
somehow. I cleaned out all the food I had in the house,
purged it, used up all the money I had going out again and
again and again to buy more. Back and forth and back and
forth from the shop to the toilet for maybe three, four days.
Trying to feel numb. Just on autopilot, like I was...
possessed, and...

By four in the morning on the last day I was vomiting blood.
I thought that was probably... it. So I just lay down next to
the toilet. That way if someone found me they wouldn't have
to carry my body down the stairs. But then a few hours later,
I woke up. Phone ringing. Not dead after all. It was Gemma,
said she was sorry about before but she'd had an emergency
shift come up – she's an ICU nurse – and could I take Molly to
her GCSE Biology exam. I should have said no obviously.
I should have said Gemma can you call me an ambulance
please, can you call me a doctor or a policeman or a fucking –
priest, but I was too proud or too ashamed so I dragged myself
out and drove round her house, must have stunk, hadn't

showered in four days, lashings of deodorant on to cover up
the smell, sunglasses on because I've burst a blood vessel in
my eye making myself sick but Gemma doesn't notice or if
she does she doesn't ask questions and then Molly gets in the
car all chirpy and clean – you know those people who always
look clean? Like they never piss or shit or sweat – and
suddenly I feel this… overwhelming rage towards her. Hatred,
almost. Because she's so clean. And while we're driving she's
yammering away to herself about the fucking kidney and how
that works and I'm just getting angrier and angrier and I'm
trying to focus on the road but everything looks blurry because
my eyes are full of these angry tears and suddenly I feel like
my brain's short-circuiting and I've forgotten who I am and
what I'm doing and I guess I must have blacked out for half
a second or something because I lost control of the car and
crashed into a tree.

It sounds worse than it was. It was a very small tree. I only
smashed up the left headlight. But when I came round and
realised what had happened… I shat myself.

SAM. Yeah. That must have been pretty scary.

ZOE. No. *I shat myself.*

This is what starts to happen. You fuck up your insides so
bad your stomach falls out your arsehole every time you put
something in your mouth, or even worse it forgets how to
digest anything at all so whatever you do eat just sits there,
rotting, until you throw it all back up whether you want to
or not –

SAM. Alright alright Jesus.

ZOE. I'm just telling you.

SAM. Why?

Pause.

ZOE. When I was your age I thought it would all be terribly
grand and romantic. Withering away into oblivion while
everyone stood round the bed crying. But it turns out it's

a lot more slow and festering than that. And I just feel like that's something you should know, before –

SAM. Well I'll be fine, so.

ZOE looks at her, scrutinising. SAM holds her gaze evenly.

ZOE. Okay.

ZOE gets up. She grabs her tobacco from the counter and goes to leave. SAM watches her, conflicted.

SAM. Can I have a fag?

ZOE turns.

ZOE. You – what?

No.

SAM. I can pay you. I've got a pound.

ZOE. I don't want a – where's this coming from? You don't even smoke.

SAM. So?

ZOE. So you shouldn't start. I don't know if you've heard but it's actually really bad for you.

SAM. You do it.

ZOE. Exactly. I'm an adult and you should know better.

SAM. I'm an adult, will you please / stop saying

ZOE. Okay well if you're an adult why don't you go out and buy your own? No one's stopping you.

SAM. I can't.

ZOE. You get unsupervised leave.

SAM. I don't have any ID, I never learnt how to drive.

ZOE. Well I can't help you, I'm sorry.

SAM. ...Fine.

Beat.

ZOE. Look if you're trying to kill your appetite / or something

SAM. I don't want it because of that, not everything's about that.

ZOE. Why d'you want it then?

SAM. Because I've never done it before. I've never smoked, I've never had a drink, I've never had sex, I've never even kissed anyone on the lips and now I'm going somewhere with a load of normal people who'll have already done all this stuff.

ZOE. Not necessarily.

SAM. Come on.

ZOE. Plenty of eighteen-year-olds haven't had sex.

SAM. Yeah but not for the reasons I haven't, not because the idea of someone even finding them attractive makes them want to die because it means they look healthy and normal and not like a… and this is what my mum always said to me, boys aren't going to fancy you when you look like that Sam, as if that isn't half the point and now I look normal and I'll have to *act* normal because everyone will think I *am* normal and –

ZOE. But you don't have to do anything you don't want to do.

SAM. But I do want to. I *want* to want to. I haven't even been to a party since my cousin's thirteenth birthday when we went rollerblading and I wasn't even allowed to join in.

ZOE *debates with herself.*

ZOE. Alright, fine. You can have *one*, that's it. But don't tell anyone where you got it.

ZOE *hands* SAM *a pre-rolled cigarette and a lighter.* SAM *looks at them for a second, then sticks the cigarette in her mouth and lights it.*

What – are you insane?! You can't do it in here!

Too late, SAM*'s taken a drag and started coughing.* ZOE *hauls her over over to the window.*

Jesus, keep it down would you!

SAM. I'm fine, I'm – (*Coughs.*)

ZOE. You need to suck, okay – suck, get it in your mouth, then breathe in. Here.

ZOE demonstrates, blowing smoke out the window. SAM copies – coughs again.

SAM. I just need to get used to it.

ZOE. Don't get used to it for god's sake, you have enough problems as it is.

She snatches the cigarette back, stubs it and chucks it out the window. Spritzes some air freshener to cover the smell.

There, you happy now? I can't help you with the drinking and the drugs and the – kissing, I'm afraid.

SAM. Ugh no thanks.

ZOE (*mock offence*). Well don't say it like that, fucking hell. That's rude.

SAM (*laughing*). I didn't mean it like…

ZOE. Give me some of that gum. (*Off* SAM*'s silence.*) Don't play dumb, I saw you chewing it.

SAM throws the packet to ZOE.

How did you get this in here anyway?

SAM. Snuck it in my bra when I came back from leave. It was Mike on the desk and I knew he wouldn't go there.

ZOE stares at her for a second, then laughs.

What?

ZOE. Nothing.

SAM (*sheepish smile*). Go on, what?

ZOE. No, just – you're very surprising, you know that? When you got here I thought you were all meek and mild and yes sir no sir. But you're a proper little rebel aren't you?

SAM (*good-natured*). Piss off.

ZOE. No, it's good. It's nice to be surprised.

They lapse into a comfortable silence as ZOE *chews.*

SAM. How come you said 'I don't any more'?

About your sister. I said I didn't know you had a twin and you said 'I don't any more'.

ZOE. Not something you can really come back from, is it? I could have killed her kid.

SAM. But it was an accident.

A silence. ZOE *becomes solemn.*

ZOE. I should clean.

She gets up.

SAM *is thrown by her sudden change of mood.*

SAM. I'm sorry –

ZOE. Can you move this stuff.

SAM *comes over and takes her drawing and pencils off the table.*

ZOE *starts cleaning.*

SAM *doesn't know what to say. She senses this is her cue to go but doesn't want to leave.*

She goes over to the CD player and puts on a Talking Heads song – 'Road to Nowhere' again, or 'Burning Down the House'.

She picks up a cloth and starts wiping down the table.

What are you doing?

SAM. Helping.

ZOE. You don't have to –

SAM. I know I don't.

ZOE *stands watching her for a moment, bemused. Then resumes cleaning.*

They clean in vaguely tense silence for a bit.

SAM *starts moving to the music, wiping the table to the rhythm of the song, trying to make* ZOE *laugh.*

It works.

SAM *does it more, until* ZOE *joins in.*

They clean and dance. This builds, becoming gradually more energetic and rambunctious, a kind of release. It might end with SAM *flicking water at* ZOE, *and* ZOE *chasing* SAM *round the table.*

When this reaches its height, LEANNE *enters. They don't notice her.*

LEANNE. Hey.

Hey.

HEY.

They abruptly stop. ZOE *rushes to turn off the music.* SAM *is breathing hard.*

What the hell is going on?

ZOE. We were just cleaning.

LEANNE. Why's the window open?

ZOE. We were hot.

LEANNE. Yeah I'll bet you were. What's that in your mouth?

Beat.

ZOE. Nothing.

LEANNE. I can see you have something in there, what is it?

ZOE *spits the gum out into her hand.*

For christ's sake, where did you get that?

SAM. It's –

ZOE. Boots.

LEANNE. What?

ZOE. Boots.

LEANNE. *Boots?*

ZOE. It's nicotine gum, I'm trying to quit.

LEANNE. Where's the / rest of it?

ZOE. They didn't have / any patches so

LEANNE. Where's the rest of it?

ZOE. That was my last piece.

LEANNE. Is that true?

ZOE. Yes.

LEANNE. If you're lying to me –

ZOE. I'm not lying to you.

LEANNE. Well I'm gonna have to search your room anyway.

ZOE. Knock yourself out. Long as you're not too busy.

LEANNE (*to* SAM). We're in room two.

    Sam.

    SAM *gathers up her drawing. She shoots* ZOE *a sheepish smile or a mouthed 'thanks' behind* LEANNE*'s back.* ZOE *smirks.*

    LEANNE *turns around –* SAM *hurries out.*

    LEANNE *turns back.*

    Look, Zoe.

ZOE. Leanne.

LEANNE. I know you and me haven't always seen eye to eye. But I can see that you've been trying really hard, these last few months. Just don't fuck it up this time.

ZOE. Should watch your language there.

    LEANNE *leaves.*

Scene Three

The next day.

The same gentle classical music from the first scene plays.

MIKE *is setting the table for lunch, placing juices and cling-filmed balls of dried fruit next to each placemat according to the meal plans listed in his folder.*

MARA *is stood watching him do it, jiggling one leg.*

After a few moments, ZOE *bursts in with* SAM.

ZOE. Are foxes dogs?

MIKE. Pardon?

ZOE. Foxes, are they dogs?

MIKE.…Is this a joke?

ZOE. It's a serious question.

MIKE. Well… no. They're foxes.

ZOE. No no, you know how a wolf's a dog, like it's in the same family or whatever. Are foxes dogs?

MIKE. I suppose?

ZOE. Told you. It's bitch.

SAM. It's definitely not bitch.

MIKE. Sorry what are you talking about?

ZOE. Five letters, female fox, second letter's I.

MIKE. / Right, okay.

SAM. It's not bitch, I do know it, I just can't think of the word.

MIKE. I agree, I don't think it's…

ZOE. You can say it Mike. It's a technical term, we won't be offended.

MIKE. Bitch.

ZOE. What did you just call me??

MIKE. / Ha ha.

SAM. I don't even think foxes are dogs.

ZOE. Well they're not cats are they?

SAM. Yeah but there's more than – horses aren't cats but they're definitely not dogs.

MIKE. Have you got any other letters?

ZOE. No but you might know this one. Former England cricket captain, somebody Hussain.

MIKE. Oh! Er… oh god, what's he called …

SAM.…Saddam.

ZOE. What?!

MIKE (*laughs*). No.

ZOE. Saddam Hussein?!

SAM. Well I don't know who he is! I've just heard the name.

MIKE. Saddam Hussein was the – war in Iraq.

SAM. Oh.

ZOE. Bloody hell. Thought you were meant to be a learned scholar.

SAM. Okay well I'm not doing History.

ZOE. Fuck me, *history*. That's *history* to her. How depressing is that. I swear that was like five years ago.

SAM. It was literally before I was born.

ZOE. Don't tell me that, I don't want to hear that.

MIKE. It's Nasser. Nasser Hussain.

ZOE. How d'you spell it?

MIKE. N-A-double-S-E-R.

ZOE. No, that doesn't fit.

MIKE. What?

ZOE (*handing him the book*). The second letter's U, see?

    NAZIA *enters*.

    Oi Naz, what do you call a female fox?

NAZIA. What?

SAM. It's not bitch is it?

MIKE. No look, that's wrong. The actress who played
    Cleopatra was Elizabeth Taylor.

ZOE. What have I put?

MIKE. Elizabeth Hurley.

ZOE. Who's Elizabeth Hurley then?

MIKE. She's the one who went out with what's-his-name. The
    posh one with floppy hair. From *Notting Hill*.

SAM. Hugh Grant.

ZOE. So you've heard of Hugh Grant.

    SAM *flips* ZOE *off*. ZOE *sticks her tongue out, or does
    a scandalised gasp*.

    LEANNE *enters*.

LEANNE. Let's take seats please.

MIKE. Do you want crisps or chocolate for your afters Nazia?

NAZIA. Ready salted.

ZOE. Right, eleven down.

MIKE. Sam?

SAM. Er – same.

ZOE. 'It has an explosive opening.' What the hell does that mean?

SAM. A bomb?

ZOE. No, that's too short.

SAM. A star. The universe.

ZOE. It's seven letters.

SAM. Maybe a film? Like an action one.

ZOE. Nazia any ideas?

NAZIA (*listless*). I dunno. A bum.

ZOE. Yes very funny.

SAM. Could be bumhole, that's seven.

ZOE. It's not gonna be bum-*hole*, is it. It's a proper book this.
It's the *Guardian*.

SAM. Well it fits!

ZOE. Very immature. You should tell her off for that.

MIKE. Alright / can we

ZOE. Anyway a bumhole *is* an explosive opening, it doesn't
have one.

MIKE. Can we cool it with the explosive-bumhole chat before
lunch please.

ZOE. She started it!

LEANNE *re-enters with two more plates of food for* MARA
and SAM.

LEANNE. Let's put that away now, come on.

*As the patients sit down, they do a sort of ritual of tying back
their hair, turning out their pockets, rolling up their sleeves.*

SAM. Can we change the   MARA (*to* LEANNE). This is
music today?   on my dislikes list.

ZOE. To what?   LEANNE. What is?

SAM. I dunno. Something a   MARA. The tomato.
bit less…
                                                  LEANNE *checks her
ZOE. *One Flew Over the*   *folder.*
Cuckoo's Nest?

SAM. Boring.

MIKE. That is a group decision I'm afraid. If you want you can table it in Community.

SAM. Can't we just decide now?

ZOE. What, and miss out on all the tedious bureaucracy?

LEANNE (*to* MARA). One minute.

LEANNE *exits with* MARA*'s plate.*

MIKE. I'll make sure it's on the agenda for you.

ZOE. Oh don't bother. I've brought this up like six times already. They never change it.

SAM. How come?

ZOE. Some people find it 'soothing', apparently.

MIKE. Nazia. Hands.

NAZIA, *who had her hands in her lap, puts them on the table.*

Thank you.

ZOE. You know you could at least get a new CD player. That one's been skipping since the last time I was here. Can you pass the salt?

SAM. Or you could get an Alexa.

ZOE. Ha! Yeah right.

MIKE. Bit too expensive with our funding.

ZOE. That's a lie, it's because they don't want us asking her 'unhelpful questions' like, Alexa how many calories are in a baked potato. As if we don't already know.

SAM. Seriously?

ZOE. We had big argument about it once, it took up the whole hour. And we never got onto my item about the broken light in the bathroom, which has also never been fixed by the way –

SAM. VIXEN!

ZOE (*jumping*). Christ.

SAM. Sorry sorry, it's – a female fox, I've just remembered, it's a vixen.

MIKE. That's it.

ZOE. Vixen? No.

SAM. It definitely is.

ZOE. We'll have to agree to disagree.

SAM. What do you mean? That's right!

MIKE. She knows, she's winding you up.

ZOE. You know speaking of foxes I learnt something interesting the other day. They're actually very unfairly maligned animals. Penguins on the other hand – evil.

MIKE. Nazia.   SAM. Evil?

NAZIA *puts her hands on the table again.*

ZOE. They're paedophiles and they have sex with other dead penguins.

SAM (*laughing*). What?!   MIKE (*disapproving*). Zoe.

ZOE. It's true, I saw it in a documentary!

MIKE. Yes but it's not appropriate dinner-table chat is it.

ZOE. Why not?

MIKE. Because it might be a sensitive subject for some people.

LEANNE *returns with* MARA's *plate.*

ZOE. Sorry, for who among us is penguin necrophilia a sensitive subject?

MIKE. You know what I mean.

ZOE. Fine, I'll trigger warning my animal facts in future –

MARA. What's this?

Beat.

LEANNE. Pardon?

MARA. What's this, here.

LEANNE. It's an extra potato wedge.

MARA. I can see that. What's it doing on my plate?

MIKE. What's the matter?

LEANNE. She told me tomato was on her dislikes list.

MARA. It is.

LEANNE. So the potato wedge is there to replace it. It's an equivalent.

MARA. But it's not equivalent. It's at least seventy calories more.

MIKE. No numbers at the table please.

MARA. But it's true.

LEANNE. The kitchen staff know what they're doing okay. They've told me it's an equivalent.

MARA. They obviously don't because it's not. (*Re: the other patients*.) Ask them.

Awkward pause.

Fine, bring me back the tomato.

LEANNE. I can't do that.

MARA. Why?

LEANNE. Because it's on your dislikes list.

MARA. I don't care. I'm not having that.

ZOE. You won't eat it anyway, what difference does it make?

MIKE. Zoe.

ZOE. / What?

LEANNE. Look, it's not an exact science –

MARA. So they know what they're doing or it's not an exact science? Which is it?

LEANNE. We're not gonna split hairs with you on this.

MARA *shoves her plate off the table onto the floor.*

A silence.

Should I –

MIKE (*to* MARA). Do you want me to bring you it in Ensure? Would that make it easier?

LEANNE. That's not really the / protocol

MIKE. Mara?

She ignores him.

(*To* LEANNE, *exiting.*) It's fine.

He leaves.

LEANNE *sits down.*

LEANNE. Alright everyone, let's try to stay focused. Focused on the task at hand.

NAZIA *is cutting her peas in half.*

Everything alright today Nazia? You seem quiet.

NAZIA *shrugs, keeps cutting up the peas.*

How was your overnight leave?

NAZIA. Fine.

LEANNE. You get up to anything fun?

NAZIA. No.

A silence. Her knife scrapes against the plate.

LEANNE. Try to stop that.

Pause.

ZOE (*forced levity*). You know what, I think you should bring up the music. In Community. I'll back you up. I'm also sick of this Classic FM shit.

SAM. ... Right.

MIKE *returns with a glass and a bit of Ensure, which he sets in front of* MARA.

ZOE. We could do themes, couldn't we? Make a whole thing of it. We could have a rota! Eighties Tuesdays. Britpop Fridays. I think it'd be a laugh –

MARA. What the fuck is this?

ZOE (*putting her cutlery down*). Jesus.

MARA. This isn't right. This is too much.

MIKE. It's a standard meal.

MARA. What's this extra then? Why's it filled up to the top?

MIKE. It's not extra, it's just because it's in a smaller glass.

MARA. Then go and get the bigger glass and put it in there.

MIKE. I'm not gonna do that.

MARA (*getting up*). Fine, I'll do it myself.

LEANNE. Mara, no.

MARA. Why, because you know I'm right?

LEANNE. We're not getting drawn into this okay, we're not going to negotiate with your illness.

MARA. What if it was less? Would you negotiate with me then?

MIKE. It's the same amount as always, I promise you.

MARA. I'm not blind, I can see that it's more!

LEANNE. Mike knows what he's / doing.

MARA. This is not five hundred mil!

LEANNE. Please, you know the rule. No numbers at the / dinner table

MARA. Fuck the rule! You don't even follow your own rules!

LEANNE. Just try to calm down. Mara.	MARA (*to* ZOE, SAM *and* NAZIA). Tell them! Tell them I'm not making it up! Look, you can see!

MIKE. Stop it please. This isn't fair.

MARA. No it isn't fucking fair! (*Re:* SAM.) How come she doesn't get this?

SAM. What?

MARA. We're meant to be on the same meal plan and you're making me have more!

ZOE. Leave her / out of it!

MARA. And she's got ready-salted crisps and she's only fucking picked them because there's less calories in them than anything else!

ZOE. JUST SHUT UP WOULD YOU.

LEANNE. Zoe!

ZOE. Like she has any leg to stand on talking about what's fucking fair!

LEANNE. You're inflaming the situation.	MARA. I'm not having it.
	MIKE. Mara, listen to me.
ZOE. You and her need to realise she's not the only one suffering!	MARA. I don't care what you say, I'm not having it!
LEANNE. We know that but carrying on like this isn't helpful for anyone.	MIKE. Let's go upstairs somewhere quiet.
	MARA. No.
ZOE. Well some fucking help you're giving the rest of us, running around after her twenty-four-seven and acting like we don't even exist all because she's hellbent on being the SICKEST ONE HERE.	MIKE. Now, please, let's go.
	MARA. I'm not going anywhere with you, you're not putting that inside me!
	MIKE. Mara –
	MARA. You're not putting it inside me! You're not putting it inside me! YOU'RE NOT PUTTING IT INSIDE ME!

MARA *throws her Ensure over* MIKE *and runs out of the room.*

MIKE/LEANNE. Mara! MARA! STOP! MARA!

MIKE *and* LEANNE *run out after her.*

ZOE. Are you serious?! You're just gonna leave us here?! On our own?!

Oh well that's great! I'll just clean this shit up again then shall I?! And you can hope none of us lob our food out the fucking window – !

SAM *slams out of her seat and leaves.*

Sam –

But she's gone.

For fuck's sake…

After a moment, ZOE *carries on eating, angrily cutting up her food.*

NAZIA *bursts into tears.*

Oh god, not you as well.

Look she kicks off all the time, you can't let it upset you.

NAZIA. It's not that.

ZOE. What is it then?

Pause.

NAZIA. He's gone.

ZOE. Who?

NAZIA. Étienne.

ZOE. Gone where?

NAZIA. He's *gone*. He's left me.

ZOE. What? When?

NAZIA. Last night.

ZOE.... Shit. What happened?

> NAZIA *shrugs, crying.*

> Well... what did he say?

NAZIA. Nothing.

ZOE. What, he didn't say *anything*? He just left? Just like that?

NAZIA. He wants kids. I don't know. I can't, probably.

ZOE. Right, but... surely he already knew that? Why all of
a sudden –

NAZIA. I don't know, okay? I don't... fuck.

> NAZIA *starts trying to pull off her engagement ring.*

ZOE. Well... maybe you can't have them *now*. But you could
do. You're... you know. Or you could adopt.

NAZIA. Yeah, right. I can't even look after myself.

ZOE. He might change his mind then.

NAZIA. He won't.

ZOE. He might. People do, don't they. About kids.

NAZIA. Stupid fucking fat *cunt* hands.

ZOE. Stop it, you're gonna hurt yourself.

NAZIA. *Good.*

> God, it's not *fair*. *He made* me come here. He said he was
> gonna leave me if I didn't come here, he said I'd rather leave
> you than bury you, if that's where this is going, and now
> he's... it's not *fair*. I did all this for him, and now look at me.

ZOE. But you can't do it for him, that's not how it works.

NAZIA. I can't even get the *fucking* ring off.

ZOE. Look, you –

> SAM *re-enters with a half-packed bag. She starts hunting
> round the room.*

> What are you doing?

SAM. Have you seen my book?

ZOE. What?

SAM. My Nietzsche book. I need it.

ZOE. Why?

   Sam what are you doing?

SAM. What's it look like? I'm going.

   ZOE *laughs, bewildered.*

ZOE. What? What do you mean you're going? Going where?

SAM. I don't know. Home. Hull. I don't know.

ZOE (*going to her*). Oh come on, don't be daft.

SAM (*throwing her off*). Get off me.

ZOE. Whoa. Calm down.

SAM. I'm calm.

ZOE. Just think about this properly alright.

NAZIA. For fuck's *sake*.

ZOE (*shut up a second*).   SAM. I've thought about it.
   Nazia.

ZOE. You can't go if you don't even know where you're going!

   Is this because of Mara? You can't let her ruin this for you,
   you have to just ignore it.

SAM. Like you did just now?

ZOE. That – I was trying to protect you!

SAM. I don't need you to protect me. Anyway it's not just
   Mara. It's everything, it's all of it. It's her with the pacing
   and the exercise –

ZOE. / Come on, she's upset.

SAM. And the standing around and cutting her fucking peas in
   half, I'm sorry but I can't take it, I need to go, I need to be
   around – people.

ZOE. What do you mean 'people'?

SAM. People my own age, *normal* people who do *normal* things and – (*To* NAZIA.) CAN YOU STOP PACING?!

NAZIA. I'm sorry you're a bit fed up Sam but my whole fucking future's just gone to shit!

SAM. Yeah well mine won't.

ZOE (*chastising*). Sam!

NAZIA. Fuck this.

    NAZIA *leaves*.

SAM. The longer I stay here the worse it gets. You were right. They suck you in.

ZOE. What? That – no. Don't listen to what I said, I was being an idiot, I didn't mean it.

SAM. Why did you say it then?

ZOE. I was trying to upset you.

SAM. What? Why?!

ZOE. Because I'm a horrible self-loathing piece of shit! I don't know! Don't listen to me – I mean listen to me now, don't listen to what I said before.

SAM. It's too late.

ZOE. Sam –

SAM. You were right, you were *right* and I'm not gonna hang around and let it happen to me. I'm not gonna be the frog. Where's Leanne?

ZOE. Just listen to me / for one second

SAM. I need my contraband box. (*Calling off.*) Leanne! I need my box!

ZOE. Sam for Christ's sake stop it!

SAM (*calling off*). Leanne!

ZOE. I'm sorry but I can't let you go!

SAM (*calling off*). LEANNE.

ZOE. I'LL TELL THEM.

Pause.

SAM. What?

You'll tell them *what*?

ZOE. I heard you. In the toilet.

SAM. I don't know what you're talking about.

ZOE. Give it up.

SAM. I don't know what you're talking about.

ZOE. You were making yourself sick.

SAM. No I wasn't.

ZOE. I heard you.

SAM. You must be hearing things because I don't do that, I've never done that.

ZOE. Then why are you smiling?

SAM. Because you're being – ridiculous, you're actually being insane!

ZOE. There's no point lying to me.

SAM. Lying to *you*? / Who are *you*?

ZOE. This isn't about me or Nazia or Mara, it's about how when you walk out the door you'll collapse straight back into your illness and that's exactly why you want to go.

SAM. No it isn't, I'm going because I actually *want* to get better.

ZOE. You can't kid a kidder Sam.

SAM. Jesus you sound like Leanne. You sound like my *mum*.

ZOE. You know what, you're right, you're not a child any more, and they're a lot more willing to let adults die than kids.

SAM. Oh my god.

ZOE. No one can make you do anything now, no one's gonna swoop in and save you until you've almost hit the fucking ground. Do you want to end up dead? Is that what you want?

SAM. You know what, you – you don't know what you're talking about, you're not inside my head!

ZOE. Oh I don't know? I've been there a thousand times!

SAM. Then why should I listen to you?

ZOE. Because I'm trying to help you!

SAM. Why!

ZOE. Because if I'd got help when I was your age maybe I wouldn't be in this fucking mess!

SAM. You're not trying to help me, you're trying to keep me in here with you!

ZOE. *What?*

SAM. You're hiding in here because you're terrified to leave! It's pathetic! And you hate it, don't you, you hate that other people get to go out and have lives when you've fucked up yours, you hate that other people have a future that isn't just rotting in this hell where the only thing you have to look forward to is what song you put on to clean the fucking kitchen, and I'm sorry for you, I really am sorry that that's the way it's all worked out but I'd *rather* fucking die than stay here and turn into you!

The dust settles on this.

SAM's rage subsides and is replaced by shame.

Heavy silence.

SAM picks up her bag and leaves.

Hold on ZOE alone.

Eviscerated.

Blackout.

Interval.

82

ACT THREE

Whenever we're ready – blackout.

In the darkness, a sense of something chaotic, evil, then, abruptly –

Scene One

Lights up.

The dining-meeting room.

MIKE *and* LEANNE.

Folders open on the table.

This is the end of a long and heated discussion.

MIKE. I think it's rash.

LEANNE. Rash?

MIKE. It's way too fucking – abrupt. It's too sudden.

LEANNE. I don't see what choice we have.

MIKE. We have to keep trying, / we can't just

LEANNE. Mike what we've been trying clearly isn't working.

MIKE. But this is what I'm telling you. It *was* working, things *were* going well, for a / long time

LEANNE. But how do we know that?

MIKE. What?

LEANNE. How do we know that if she hasn't been honest with us?

MIKE. I – we don't know that for sure.

LEANNE. Come on.

MIKE. We don't know she's been lying to us / the whole time.

LEANNE. She's definitely been lying by omission if she hasn't lied to our faces.

MIKE. Then we should give her another chance to tell the truth.

LEANNE. Mike...

MIKE. We have to take some responsibility for how things have played out here.

LEANNE. That doesn't change the situation now, we can't drag this out forever.

MIKE. But we shouldn't jump the gun either.

LEANNE. There's jumping the gun and there's pissing about at the starting line till / our bloody legs fall off.

MIKE. But maybe this is just	LEANNE. How can it be
a blip, maybe if we could	a blip if it's been going on
get her to explain this	as long as it has? You're
backslide then we can	not being rational about
figure out a way of helping	this, alright, we need to
her turn it around before	stop kidding ourselves that
we –	she's – OKAY, okay.

Beat. LEANNE *pinches the bridge of her nose like she's nursing a tension headache.*

MIKE *compulsively and absent-mindedly tightens his watch-strap around his wrist. He notices* LEANNE *noticing him doing it. He stops.*

LEANNE. Look. You might think I'm Nurse Ratched –

MIKE. I never / said that

LEANNE. But I am actually thinking about her best interests here. I know you find it hard sometimes not to get... emotionally involved –

MIKE. What's that supposed to mean?

LEANNE. I'm not having a go. I do too. I know it might not look like it, but I do. But at the end of the day you've got to be realistic. If you never take a hard line then it doesn't help anyone, and I really don't think this soft-touch, pussyfooting round the issue is helping her any more.

MIKE. I'm not 'pussyfooting', I'm trying to build an empathetic therapeutic relationship with her.

LEANNE. Fine, but you've got to accept that if someone's not willing to work with you then you can't –

MIKE. Yes I do know that Leanne, I've been in this a lot longer than you have.

Sorry. That was.

It's about trust. Okay? She has to trust us.

LEANNE. Do you trust her? Cos it's a two-way street.

Pause.

MIKE. Let's just bring her in.

LEANNE. I'll be bad cop, shall I?

LEANNE *exits.*

After a few moments she re-enters, followed by ZOE.

Beat.

ZOE. Christ, who died?

LEANNE. Do you want to sit down.

ZOE *sits – tilts her chair back on two legs.*

LEANNE *slides a sheet of paper across the table.*

ZOE. What?

LEANNE. Look.

ZOE. I've looked.

LEANNE. Don't be combative.

ZOE. I'm not being / combative

LEANNE. This is the sixth week in a row you've lost weight on leave. Is there anything you want to say about that?

Beat.

LEANNE *slides more sheets across the table.*

Here are the meal diaries you've been filling in. These two things can't both be true, can they? That would defy the laws of physics. So either you've been making up the diaries or finding ways to get rid of what you've put in.

ZOE. I haven't done that.

LEANNE. Done what?

ZOE. I haven't purged.

LEANNE. You haven't been vomiting.

ZOE. No.

LEANNE. Are your bloods gonna show us that or are they gonna show us something else?

ZOE. I haven't been vomiting.

LEANNE. Can you put the chair down.

ZOE *crashes her chair back onto four legs.*

You haven't been abusing any medication?

ZOE. No.

LEANNE. Over-exercising?

ZOE. No.

LEANNE. So you've been lying on the diaries.

ZOE. No.

LEANNE (*to* MIKE). You see? What she's saying doesn't make sense.

ZOE. Can you not talk about me in the third person.

MIKE. She's right Zoe. It doesn't add up.

ZOE. I'm still a healthy weight.

LEANNE. You were a healthy weight when you got here and you were very far from healthy.

ZOE. Exactly so it doesn't mean anything.

LEANNE. You're manipulating the conversation now.

ZOE. No I'm not, it's a statement of fact. I'm still a healthy weight.

LEANNE. So that's the plan? To keep this up until you're not?

ZOE. You're putting words in my mouth.

LEANNE. Put it in your words then.

A silence.

Okay, I'll start: we think you're hiding something. You're withdrawn, reticent.

ZOE. Reticent?

MIKE. Quiet.

ZOE. I know what it means.

LEANNE. You're not engaged with the programme.

ZOE. That's not true.

LEANNE. You've given the same Helpful Thought three days in a row.

ZOE. God forbid, the same Helpful Thought!

LEANNE. It's important Zoe.

ZOE. Is that what it all comes down to?

LEANNE. No. In fact you're hardly speaking in groups at all.

ZOE. Maybe I've run out of things to say.

LEANNE. That's not like you.

ZOE. Is that a dig?

LEANNE. It's an observation.

ZOE. What do you want from me? There's only so many times
you can have the same conversation.

LEANNE. So you can imagine how we feel.

Pause.

ZOE. I walk. On leave. Not to pace, not for exercise, just…
I can't keep food in the house. So every time I need to eat
I have to walk to the shop.

MIKE. So you've been getting the urge to –

ZOE. Yes.

MIKE. Binge. But you haven't?

ZOE. No.

MIKE. And you haven't purged.

ZOE. I just told you, no.

MIKE. That's good. (*To* LEANNE.) That's good.

LEANNE. You couldn't drive?

ZOE. What?

LEANNE. You couldn't drive to the shop.

ZOE. I don't drive any more.

LEANNE. Get the bus?

ZOE. There isn't one.

LEANNE. Taxi?

ZOE. What am I a fucking millionaire?

LEANNE. Watch the language.

ZOE. How am I supposed to afford six taxis a day on disability?
It barely covers my rent.

LEANNE. Okay well unless this shop's ten miles away it wouldn't fully explain these kinds of drops. You understand there's a limit to how long we can let this carry on? You can't be in here going backwards like this. We can't just go round in circles forever.

Beat.

Look, we've had a long... discussion, about this. And we think –

MIKE (*abruptly*). We think you should stay here for a few weeks.

LEANNE *looks at him, surprised.*

Over the weekends I mean. We can recommend that to Dr Murphy in your review, keep an eye on your intake, put in place some strategies to help manage these urges you've been having. I also think we should suggest taking you off choosing privilege –

ZOE. Oh, what!

MIKE. Get you back on a set meal plan and reintroduce the Ensure / as a contingency

ZOE. No no no I'm not going back to the Ensure.

MIKE. You won't have to if you complete in solids but it'll be there as a last resort. But we need to start reversing these losses as soon as possible and I really think this is the best option to turn things around.

What do you think?

ZOE (*mumbles*)....Fine.

MIKE. Pardon?

ZOE. Yes. I consent.

MIKE *looks at* LEANNE.

LEANNE. That's that then.

She gets up. MIKE *follows.*

At the door, LEANNE *says something to* MIKE *that neither* ZOE *nor the audience can hear.*

LEANNE *exits.*

MIKE *turns back into the room.*

MIKE. Right, are you gonna tell me what's really going on?

I'm really worried about you Zoe.

ZOE. Spare me another interrogation. I just said.

MIKE. Not the weight loss, all of it. I haven't seen you like this in a long time. You're isolated. You won't talk to anyone. When you are here you're always in your room.

ZOE. Thought you said that wasn't 'necessarily sinister'.

MIKE. Leanne's right. It's not like you.

ZOE. I'm just doing what you told me to. Focusing on myself.

Pause. ZOE *picks at the table.*

MIKE. Has this got something to do with Sam?

ZOE. What?

MIKE. It hasn't escaped my notice that you've been on this spiral ever since she left.

ZOE. Exactly. She's not here, why would it be about her?

MIKE. So you acknowledge there's an 'it'. That's a start.

ZOE. This table's filthy. Who wiped this down?

MIKE. I know you think we messed that whole thing up.

ZOE. I never said that.

MIKE. Well I know things were very difficult round then, with Mara –

ZOE. Oh, *Mara*. That's all sorted now, isn't it? Little Miss Sunshine now. Is she on Cleaning Duty by the way? / Or Nazia?

MIKE. I'm just saying, if you still feel angry about all that, you can tell me.

ZOE. Angry at who? At Mara?

MIKE. At me, at us, about that whole / situation

ZOE. I'm not angry at Mara, no. I'm happy for her. You think she's cured then good for her.

MIKE. I don't think / she's *cured*

ZOE. Just seems a bit suspicious if you ask me. One minute you've got her on bed rest being held down and sedated three times a day and then all of a sudden she comes downstairs, nice as pie, eats all her Coco Pops with fifteen minutes to spare – (*Insipid voice.*) 'yesterday I found it helpful listening to the birdies outside the window because it reminded me how beautiful the world can be'. I mean what did you give her up there, a fucking exorcism?

MIKE. It was a much slower process than that.

ZOE. Seemed pretty bloody swift to me. Got another one up there now thought right? That's how it works. The conveyor belt. What's her name again? Susan?

MIKE. Suzanne.

ZOE. When's she coming down?

MIKE. I get how the whole Mara thing might seem sudden but that doesn't mean it isn't real. Sometimes that can happen.

ZOE. Can it.

MIKE. Yes. Sometimes something just clicks and people feel ready to change.

ZOE *laughs*.

What?

ZOE. Nothing.

MIKE. Go on, what.

ZOE. You really believe that? It's that easy.

MIKE. I didn't say it was *easy*.

ZOE. So it's my fault then? For not being ready. It's my fault nothing's 'clicked'.

MIKE. No. Now *you're* putting words in *my* mouth.

ZOE. Go on then. If you're such an expert. Perform this fucking magic clicking ritual and click me.

MIKE. You know it doesn't work like that.

ZOE. Oh really? How does it work then?

MIKE. It has to come from the person.

ZOE. How convenient. I suppose that lets you off the hook.

It's not just about wanting to get better. I know you lot like to think so but it's not. Wanting it isn't enough.

MIKE. But not wanting to means you definitely won't, and I know that you do. Look, Gemma –

ZOE. Fucking hell.

MIKE. I know you don't want to talk about it but we're on a slippery slope here and I really think it might help turn things around if she was involved. She told me she's been ringing every clinic you've been in over the last ten years looking for information. She wants to help you.

ZOE. Mike, stop.

MIKE. This guilt you've tormented yourself with, at some point you're gonna have to confront it

ZOE. / Just stop it, alright

MIKE. And you don't have to do it on your own, we can support you, we can set up some family therapy sessions with her and with Molly even –

ZOE. Jesus, no!

MIKE. I know it's really tough, / but we can't carry on as we are and

ZOE. God I hate how you all say that! Have you ever shat
    yourself?

MIKE. You – what?

ZOE. Have you ever shat yourself? Have you ever binged until
    you couldn't walk and you thought your stomach would rip
    open and still not been able to stop? Have you ever vomited
    until your eyes bled and your teeth rotted out of your head?

MIKE. This isn't – / what is this?

ZOE. Do you have any idea what it's like to live with this
    fucking thing in your head, every minute of every day, just
    picking at you and picking at you and telling you what to do,
    telling you you're an evil fucking worthless piece of *shit*
    who doesn't deserve to eat, who doesn't deserve to be happy,
    who doesn't deserve to live?

MIKE. Please / just

ZOE. No?

MIKE. Just hear me out.

ZOE. Why? Because you're the professional and I'm the
    lunatic? Because you've got a degree and a folder and a
    fucking – lanyard, that means you get to stand there and tell
    me do this, do that, patronise me like I'm an idiot if I don't
    agree with you, trot out these meaningless fucking aphorisms
    when the truth is you know fuck-all, you have absolutely no
    idea how 'tough' it is because you've never / actually

MIKE (*erupting*). How do you know I haven't!

    Silence.

    MIKE *looks shocked at what he's just said.*

ZOE. What?

    Oh my god, are you serious?

    Pause.

    Yes.

Fuck.

Do they know? Leanne. The staff.

MIKE. I – of course they do, it wouldn't be ethical to hide it.

ZOE. But they still hired you?

MIKE. It was a long time ago.

ZOE. What was 'it'? Was it anorexia, bulimia, what?

MIKE. Look I'm – I'm sorry Zoe, I really shouldn't have said that.

ZOE. Why?

MIKE. Because it's not appropriate, I'm not supposed to bring my personal life into / our relationship

ZOE. Personal life? Is that what we're calling it now?

MIKE. You know what / I mean

ZOE. Well you have, so what was it?

Pause.

MIKE. I was – I was like you.

ZOE. So you had both?

MIKE. Bulimia, mostly. For about, nine years.

ZOE. Were you ever in hospital?

MIKE. No, nobody – this was a long time ago, most people didn't even think it happened to…

ZOE. Men.

MIKE. Right.

ZOE. So you were never tube-fed. That's interesting. Do you think that's why you could do it to Mara?

MIKE *is thrown.*

MIKE. I do it because it's part of the job and it keeps people alive.

ZOE. But you don't like it.

MIKE. Nobody *likes* it.

ZOE. Do you feel guilty?

MIKE. It's my job, it's a necessary part of / the job

ZOE. So are you better now?

MIKE. What?

ZOE. Are you better.

MIKE. I – obviously.

ZOE. Why obviously?

MIKE. Because I wouldn't work here if I wasn't.

ZOE. Really? The people who get better don't normally hang
    around talking to the people who don't. I should know. I mean
    shouldn't you be out there, living your life with a load of
    normal people? Why are you in here with me?

MIKE. Because I / want to

ZOE. Is it a way to hang on to it?

MIKE. What? / No!

ZOE. Or are you like one of those smackheads who can only
    stay clean when they man the reception at a rehab clinic?

MIKE (*to himself*). Christ.

ZOE. I'm genuinely asking.

MIKE. I'm here because I want to help, okay. I am actually
    trying to help you.

ZOE. So how did you do it then? How did you stop?

    Beat. MIKE *flounders.*

    Come on. You want to help, answer the question.

MIKE. I don't… I don't know.

ZOE. You don't *know*?

MIKE. I don't know how to explain it.

ZOE. Then try at least.

MIKE. But it doesn't – look if I could give you some magic formula / that would make this all go away then believe me I would but it doesn't work like that –

ZOE. I'm not *thick*, I'm not asking for a *formula*, I'm asking how *you* did it.

MIKE. But that's not gonna teach you how to do it, it has to come from you.

ZOE. Great, so we're back to this then.

MIKE. Zoe, come on. You know this, it's, it's different –

ZOE. Why? Because you're a man?

MIKE. Because it's different for everyone.

ZOE. Well that was really illuminating Mike, thanks for the help.

MIKE. I had a reason. To do it. I was more scared of dying than I was of living. I was more scared of having no life than living without... I had a reason. I don't know what else to say.

ZOE. What if you've got no reason.

MIKE. Everyone has a reason.

ZOE. That's glib bollocks. No they don't.

MIKE. Then we need to help you find one.

Will you please think about what I said? About Gemma. I'm not pushing it to harass you, I really... at some point, in the end, you have to live in the world. And one thing I do know is it's really bloody hard to do it on your own.

Pause.

ZOE. Okay.

MIKE. Okay you'll –

ZOE. I'll think about it.

MIKE. Alright. Alright.

MIKE *leaves.*

We hold on ZOE *alone for a moment, staring at nothing. Trying to resist.*

She can't.

She goes over to the CD player and puts some music on.

She turns the volume up.

She goes into the toilet.

Scene Two

Time passes. The light changes. Late-autumn sun pours in through the window and hits the wall of handprints, making them look yellow.

The music's still playing.

NAZIA *enters with a bunch of real flowers. She goes over to the table and begins arranging them in a jug.*

She looks at the chair.

A moment of inner conflict.

Then she sits down. Continues arranging the flowers.

The music player skips. NAZIA *looks at it. It goes back to normal. She returns to her flowers.*

The music starts skipping madly, playing the same minor clashing notes over and over. NAZIA *reaches over and turns it off.*

There's a coughing from the toilet, and the noise of the tap running. NAZIA *looks up.*

A few seconds pass.

MARA *enters. She's carrying Sam's left-behind copy of Nietzsche and looks very different than when we last saw her.*

MARA. Hey.

NAZIA. Hey.

MARA. Oh wow. Those are festive.

NAZIA. They're nice aren't they? My mum sent them.

MARA. Are they poinsettias?

NAZIA. Er – I dunno, are they?

MARA. They are. I don't know why I asked.

NAZIA. Right. Well, I thought they might brighten up the room.

More coughing from the toilet, then a flush, and the sound of the tap going off.

MARA *and* NAZIA *look towards it, then at each other.*

A beat in which it's clear they both know what's going on.

One of them might go to say something, but then ZOE *enters.*

MARA *and* NAZIA *break eye contact, busy themselves.* NAZIA *goes back to her flowers.* MARA *sits down and reads her book.*

Tense silence.

MARA *looks at* ZOE *out of the corner of her eye.*

ZOE *senses her gaze – looks over.* MARA *quickly looks away.*

ZOE. Where did you get that?

MARA. What?

ZOE. Where did you get that book?

MARA. It was in lost property.

LEANNE *and* MIKE *enter, wheeling one of those flipchart whiteboards.*

LEANNE. Alright everyone! Vamanos, vamanos, let's get started.

Movement as people start bringing over chairs etc.

(*Handing* MARA *some paper.*) Can you hand these out for me? No chairs today!

ZOE. We're standing up?

LEANNE. No, we're going to sit on the floor. Mix it up, bit more casual.

ZOE. The floor? Wow. Anarchy.

LEANNE. Cushions, if anybody needs cushions, if anybody wants cushions, everyone take a pen…

She chucks a pot of pens into the centre of the circle. Everyone settles.

Okay. Good afternoon everyone and welcome to Monday Group.

ALL. Good afternoon.

LEANNE. We're gonna return today to our work on Cognitive Regulation starting with an exercise called… (*Like a fanfare.*) da da-da daaa…

She flips over the whiteboard to reveal a flowchart inside a diagram of a tree.

NAZIA/MARA (*reading*). 'The Worry Tree'.

LEANNE. Yes! Now I actually think the word 'worry' sounds a bit negative and angsty and *stressy* so let's call it something else, let's call it the the the –

NAZIA. The Fear Tree?

LEANNE. Thanks Nazia, fear's still a bit – gah! – though so maybe –

ZOE (*deadpan*). The Unhelpful-Thought Tree.

LEANNE. Unhelpful is still quite *negative* so maybe the, the…

MARA. The Challenging-Thought Tree.

LEANNE. Good! I like it. (*Writing*.) The... Challenging... Thought... Tree. Great. Now the purpose of this exercise is help nip those catastrophic spirals of anxiety in the bud. To help us recognise what is and is not in our control.

ZOE. Wow, thirty-five seconds. That's got to be a record.

LEANNE. Step one is to 'notice the challenging thought'. So I'd like you all to write down a challenging thought you've been having over the past, let's say twenty-four hours.

They start writing.

Oh and make sure it's something you feel comfortable sharing with the group.

NAZIA *crosses out what she'd written down.* LEANNE *gives it a second.*

We've all got one?

VARIOUS. Yep. Yeah.

LEANNE. Excellent. Nazia, if you could start us off.

NAZIA. Do I just read it out?

LEANNE. Please.

NAZIA. 'Losing Pepper.'

LEANNE *writes 'LOSING PEPPER' on the board.*

MIKE. Can you expand on that?

NAZIA. Pepper's my dog.

LEANNE. Ooh, what kind?

NAZIA. Australian Shepherd.

LEANNE. N'aww.

NAZIA. And me and Étienne have been arguing about... custody, for when I get out of here. And I mean she's my dog really, like I'm the one who wanted her and I did everything,

I named her and fed her and walked her and picked up all her crap. He could never be arsed. And my worry is / that he's

LEANNE. 'My challenging thought' –

NAZIA. My *challenging thought* is that he's gonna take her away from me.

MARA. Why would he do that if she's your dog?

NAZIA. He thinks I can't look after her.

MARA. What? Why?

NAZIA. I dunno. Cos I'm 'mental' or whatever. He didn't come out and say it but that's the – gist.

MARA. But that's not fair, you're doing so much better.

MIKE. And it sounds like you were really good at looking after her.

NAZIA (*shrugs*). Yeah, well. S'what he said.

LEANNE. Okay, step two is to ask ourselves, can I do anything about this challenging thought? Anyone chip in, it's a group exercise.

Pause.

ZOE. Kidnap it.

MARA. You could write a letter. To Étienne.

ZOE. Dognap?

LEANNE. Ooh! Great suggestion.

ZOE. Which one.

MARA. If you're arguing, and you're not getting anywhere… I found that helpful when I was on bed rest. I'd get too angry and upset sometimes and it was like I couldn't think properly, but if I wrote things down, it helped. You could lay out all the reasons why you should keep her, he might be more responsive if it's not in the heat of the moment.

LEANNE. Excellent. Would that be helpful Nazia?

NAZIA. Maybe, yeah.

LEANNE. And is this something you can do now?

NAZIA. What, right now?

LEANNE. Yes.

NAZIA. Well, we're doing this…?

LEANNE. No. Fine. So when can you do it?

NAZIA. After? Like – four?

LEANNE. Great, so then we *schedule* it… like… so… and now we've decided *what* we're going to do and *when* we're going to do it we can let the challenging thought go and change the focus of our attention. Nazia, please rip up your thought and chuck it in the bin.

> NAZIA *does so*. LEANNE *initiates a clap* – MIKE *and* MARA *join in*.

ZOE. That's it?

LEANNE. It's hard to let the thoughts go at first but the more you practise the easier it gets. Mara next please.

MARA. Mine's a bit broad, I hope that's okay. 'Leaving.'

> LEANNE *writes 'LEAVING' on the board*.

ZOE. You're leaving?

MARA. Yeah.

ZOE. What, *leaving* leaving? When?

MARA. On Friday. I found out last week my section's been lifted and decided that's the best thing for me.

NAZIA. Wow. That's great, Mara. Congratulations.

LEANNE. Yes, brilliant news.   MIKE. Really good.

> *Maybe she gets a little round of applause.* ZOE *is perplexed.*

LEANNE. Okay, can we break this down a bit? Make it more specific?

MARA. Obviously I'm really happy to be getting out of here. No offence.

MIKE. None taken.

Chuckles round the room. It irritates ZOE. *She starts picking at the carpet.*

MARA. And like, really happy to finally have control over my life. But I suppose the idea of being at home and managing everything... I'm really determined, I'm going to do it, but yeah. It's nerve-wracking.

NAZIA. Do you live on your own?

MARA. I'm staying with my mum and dad for the first few weeks.

NAZIA. That's good. Good you'll be around people.

MARA. Yeah. I mean it's not for long, it's just while I get settled. But obviously I haven't seen anyone for a while, from like, my life, and I'm a bit nervous about how they'll react now I look... different.

MIKE. React in the sense of...

MARA. Well like my brother Dan for example, his kids – they're only five and six, they don't get it. So they'd just ask, you know – Daddy, what's wrong with Auntie Mara? Why does she look like that? She looks scary.

ZOE *starts picking harder at the carpet.*

I think Dan told them I had cancer. And like at work – I was an assistant at a pharmacy and I used to get a lot of looks, people staring, whispering behind their hands, sometimes even saying stuff to your face. One bloke told me I looked like I'd just walked out of Auschwitz, right in front of the whole queue.

LEANNE. Gosh.

MARA. It made people uncomfortable, I think. No one wants to get their medicine from someone who looks like they're dying. And part of me felt ashamed, of course, being gawped at like some sort of freak. But the sick thing is, I liked it. Or – the illness liked it. Because it meant I looked terrible. And if I looked terrible that meant I was 'succeeding', at being ill. Which is all I really cared about at the time. Because I was like… in love. With the illness. And the thing is, now people won't do that. Like my nephews, they're gonna say, oh, you look so much better now, Auntie Mar, you look normal again. Trying to be nice. And obviously there's still a part of my brain – the, the illness part, not the Mara part, that really doesn't want to look better or 'normal' and I know I obviously need to ignore that part –

LEANNE. Well maybe ignore is the wrong word because we shouldn't *ignore* the challenging thoughts, rather acknowledge them and accept them and counter them with more helpful ones. Is there anything Mara can do about this? Anyone.

Pause.

MIKE. Could you talk Dan about this beforehand? Have him tell the kids not to comment?

MARA. I dunno. He can be a bit defensive. And I don't really like making a fuss.

ZOE snorts loudly. Everyone looks at her.

LEANNE. Can you offer any advice?

ZOE looks up.

ZOE. I'm not underweight.

LEANNE. You have been in the past.

ZOE. Not for years. Not like she was. People look at me and think I'm making it up.

LEANNE. That must be challenging.

ZOE stares at her. Slightly tense pause.

MARA. Sorry. I didn't mean to say anything – upsetting.

MIKE (*to* ZOE). Maybe you can offer some more general advice.

ZOE. About what?

MIKE. Dealing with discharge. You've been in Mara's position a few times.

ZOE. Exactly, why should she listen to me?

MIKE. Maybe you could share your experience. Advise on things that help, or things to avoid.

ZOE. There's a stain.

MIKE. What?

ZOE. There's a stain, here, on the carpet.

MIKE. Try to stay engaged.

ZOE. I don't know, Mike, why don't *you* give her some advice?

Beat. LEANNE *looks at* MIKE. *He avoids her gaze.*

MIKE. I think it would be more helpful coming from you.

Beat.

ZOE. Alright. You might think it's really shit –

LEANNE. Watch the –

ZOE. You might think it's really *challenging* being in here and having no 'control' over your life, following the schedule like you're back in primary school, but out there? People say life's too short, it's not. It's too bloody long. There's too much time and too many ways to fill it, all those hours in all those days, all those choices you have to make. And you've got to hold yourself to account for those choices because you won't have teacher here to do it for you. No one breathing down your neck twenty-four-seven saying do this, eat that, sit down, stop doing that with your hands. You're on your own.

LEANNE. That's not true. You'll have your outpatient team.

ZOE. What, an hour a week with some trainee psychologist barely out of nappies? Then after six months you get palmed off on some other poor sod and you have to explain the whole sorry story all over again?

MARA. Mine aren't like that. They're good.

ZOE. Really? So how come you ended up in here?

LEANNE. I'm not / sure this is

ZOE. As for the rest of the world, normal people, sane people, yeah, they might give it all this about 'mental health', let's go for a walk and sit in a prayer circle and talk about our bloody feelings, but if you're mentally *ill*? Pfft. Forget it, they don't want to know. And sure, at first it's all very dramatic and interesting but after a while, after years – they get bored.

LEANNE. That's a very pessimistic way of looking at it.

ZOE. It's the truth. That's paramount isn't it? Telling the truth. You're on your own, and you have to take responsibility for yourself. So if I were you, I'd be very, very honest about whether I was ready for all that, or just pretending to be.

Pause.

LEANNE. Was any of that helpful?

MARA. Yeah. It was actually. Thank you.

LEANNE. Great. Do me the honours.

MARA *rips up her paper and throws it in the bin.* LEANNE *initiates a clap for her.*

NAZIA. Can I say something?

The clap dies out.

I lied before. About Pepper. A few months ago, whenever I was home on leave at the weekends or whatever – Étienne was out of the house a lot, he had to take on extra work to cover the mortgage and whenever he left I'd go out running. And I couldn't leave Pepper on her own all day because she'd get really anxious and start pooing everywhere so I used to take her out with me, for hours and hours, and...

I know I shouldn't have been doing it but I just – I needed the exercise, I had to have the exercise and she's an energetic breed, you know, I thought she'd be fine, she *seemed* fine, at first, she never whined or barked or stopped, but… after a while, she started limping. Off her back leg, like there was something wrong with her foot. And when Étienne took her to the vet they told him she had all these – lacerations, they called them, on her paws, the little pads on her paws, from over-exercise, and one of them had got infected. She was in agony. They told Étienne they thought they'd have to… amputate, and…

He wouldn't even look at me, when he got home. That was the last straw. It was the lying, I think, more than the dog. But I'd never do that again. I don't want to do that again.

Long silence.

MIKE. That was very brave of you to say, Nazia.

LEANNE. Yes. Very brave. Well done.

Pause.

We do need to carry on –

NAZIA. Yeah. Sorry. I just needed to…

LEANNE. No, of course. Thank you for sharing that. I know that must have been tough.

MIKE. We'll talk about it more later, okay?

NAZIA. Sure.

A clap. When it dies down:

LEANNE. Zoe.

ZOE. I don't get this.

LEANNE. What do you mean?

ZOE. I don't understand what we're doing.

LEANNE. We're trying to manage our challenging thoughts by determining / whether or not

ZOE. But what is this actually achieving? She's just said all that and now what, we just dismiss it and move on?

MIKE (*to* NAZIA). We're not / dismissing it Nazia

ZOE. Problem solved?

LEANNE. It's not about *solving* the problem, it's about dealing with the thoughts *surrounding* the problem.

ZOE. But what does that actually *do*?

LEANNE. It helps you manage your anxiety.

ZOE. But for *what*?

LEANNE. Why don't you just give it a go?

ZOE. Fine. Global warming.

LEANNE. I'm sorry?

ZOE. Global warming.

It's when gas gets trapped in the –

LEANNE. Yes I know what global warming is. That's a challenging thought you've had in the last twenty-four hours?

ZOE. It's a very challenging situation. I don't know if you've been watching the news.

LEANNE. Come on. Do it properly.

ZOE. I am doing it properly. That's my challenging thought.

LEANNE (*tight*)….Okay.

She writes it down.

Global… warming. Is there anything Zoe can do about this? Anyone.

Pause.

MARA. She could… recycle.

LEANNE. Good.

MARA. Use less electric. Less plastics. Buy second-hand. There's loads of things.

LEANNE. And is this something she can do now?

MARA. I suppose she can do it when she gets out. If she wants.

LEANNE. Right. So now we've identified what can be done and when it can be done, we can let the thought go and change the focus / of our attention

ZOE. But what's the point? That doesn't fix anything.

LEANNE. Like I said it's not about / fixing it

MARA. It does help though.

ZOE. No it doesn't, that's all just window-dressing, fucking –

LEANNE. Zoe.

ZOE. Meaningless busywork to make ourselves feel better. I mean it's basically too late, right? We're all fucked, the world's ending, so what's the point. Literally what is the point. What's the point of this, now? What's the point of anything?

MARA. What's the point of *anything*?

LEANNE. Right well in that case we come to the conclusion that it's not in our control and so we let the challenging thought go –

ZOE (*ripping up her bit of paper*). Oh good. That was easy! I hope you're recycling these by the way. Or not, who cares?

MIKE. Zoe come on. This isn't fair.

ZOE. I'm sorry but this is ridiculous. None of this means anything. None of this is actually *real*.

MIKE. Other people might get something out of it.

ZOE (*to* NAZIA). You found that helpful did you?

LEANNE. Let's just move on to / the next exercise

ZOE. Nazia.

NAZIA. I don't know.

ZOE. Come on!

NAZIA. I don't know, maybe, I don't know.

ZOE. She's being polite.

MIKE. She can speak for herself.

MARA. I found it helpful.

ZOE. Oh fuck off Hermione.

LEANNE. Oi!

MARA. I don't see why you have to ruin it for her –

ZOE. Wow, look who's talking!

MARA. If you don't want to take it seriously / that's your choice

LEANNE gets a message on her phone.

ZOE. How do you know I'm not taking it seriously?

MARA. Really?

ZOE. You don't know what my challenging thoughts are, you're not inside my head!

LEANNE. / Guys… Guys.

MARA. Okay well if you're really that worried about global warming maybe you can start by turning that tap off while you're in there – !

LEANNE. *Guys.*

They fall silent.

We've got a call with Mara's outpatient team.

MIKE. It's booked for five.

LEANNE. Yes well they can't do it later and they can't reschedule, it's got to be now. (*To* ZOE *and* NAZIA.) I'm sorry, we'll pick this up next time.

LEANNE, MIKE and MARA exit.

ZOE. Bye then.

ZOE gets up, agitated.

A long, awkward silence.

What.

...What.

NAZIA. I didn't say anything.

ZOE. Great. You're on her side.

NAZIA. What are you talking about? Whose side?

ZOE. I don't get this. You saw what she was like and now she's what, some beacon of recovery? Miss fucking Perfect?

NAZIA. Why do you care so much? She'll be gone soon.

ZOE. People left because of her. Because of how she carried on.

NAZIA. She was ill.

ZOE. We're all *ill.*

NAZIA. At least she's trying.

ZOE. No she isn't.

NAZIA. How do you know?

ZOE. Because I've been around the block enough to know the difference. She's just trying to get out.

NAZIA. It's a start isn't it? You know she is actually quite nice. And it helps me, seeing her. It makes it all feel a bit less fucking hopeless.

Beat.

ZOE. Look I'm sorry. I didn't mean to snap at you. And I'm sorry about your dog.

NAZIA. Don't.

ZOE. I mean it. I know what that's like, when you can't... forgive yourself.

Beat.

NAZIA. You know what's funny? It was a relief, in the end.
I did everything I could to hide it from him but when he
finally found out, it was such a relief. It's the only way I ever
could have stopped.

NAZIA *looks at her.*

A charged silence.

Then ZOE *leaves.*

NAZIA *watches her go.*

Scene Three

The Treatment Room. Early morning the next day. LEANNE
and MIKE *are present.*

ZOE *enters.*

Stops short when she sees LEANNE.

ZOE. What are you doing here?

LEANNE. Good morning to you too.

ZOE. What's going on?

LEANNE. I need to take your obs.

ZOE. You never do them now.

LEANNE. Dr Murphy wants to see them.

ZOE. Why?

LEANNE. Because she needs to.

ZOE (*about Mike*). Why can't he do it?

   Beat.

LEANNE. Is there a problem?

ZOE *takes off her dressing gown and goes over to the scale.*
LEANNE *preps the obs equipment.*

MIKE. Have you been to the toilet?

ZOE. Yes.

MIKE. Number one or / number

ZOE. Piss.

MIKE. Right. Any fluids / since?

ZOE. No.

MIKE. Step on.

ZOE *gets on the scale, facing forwards. The numbers settle. The scale beeps.*

Step off.

MIKE *writes down* ZOE*'s weight and shows it to* LEANNE. *Clear from her face it's not good news.*

LEANNE. Take a seat.

ZOE *sits.* LEANNE *takes her temperature.*

You sleep alright?

ZOE. Fine.

LEANNE. Any problems in the night?

ZOE. No.

The thermometer beeps.

LEANNE. Thirty-seven-point-four.

MIKE *writes it down.* LEANNE *starts taking her heart rate and blood pressure.* ZOE *coughs.*

That doesn't sound good. I'm guessing that's the acid reflux? Has it been getting worse recently?

ZOE. Just a smoker's cough.

LEANNE. I see. How's your attempt to quit coming along?

ZOE. What?

LEANNE. I thought you were trying to quit.

ZOE is confused.

The nicotine gum.

ZOE. Oh, yeah. I stopped.

LEANNE. I've seen you going out for –

ZOE. I stopped quitting.

LEANNE (*to* MIKE, *unstrapping the blood pressure cuff*). Heart rate's eighty-six, BP's a hundred and twelve over seventy-four.

MIKE writes it down. ZOE *gets up.*

Hang on a second.

Is everything alright with you?

ZOE. What do you mean?

LEANNE. I get the impression people are quite concerned about you.

ZOE. What people?

Beat.

LEANNE. There's nothing going on? Nothing we should know about?

ZOE. Like what?

MIKE. Nothing you haven't told us.

ZOE. No.

Beat. They watch her evenly. ZOE *laughs/smiles uncomfortably.*

No.

LEANNE. Are you sure?

ZOE. Yes.

LEANNE. You know how important it is to be honest.

ZOE. There's nothing going on.

MIKE. Because we understand how it might be difficult to say
 if –

ZOE. Fucking hell, there's nothing going on.

Pause.

LEANNE. Okay.

ZOE. Is that it?

LEANNE. That's it. Thank you.

ZOE leaves.

LEANNE and MIKE look at one another.

*A moment of suspension. Some wordless decision or
capitulation happens between them.*

Then LEANNE turns and picks up the phone.

Hi Nicki it's me. We've just had her in… (*She looks at
MIKE.*) No… Yeah… Yes, we think so too… Today?

She gets a folder down and starts rifling through it.

What time will they get here?… She will be, yes… Alright.
Thank you.

She hangs up.

A heavy silence.

I think maybe we were expecting too much.

Pause.

MIKE. I'll let her know.

Scene Four

NAZIA *and* MARA *are sat waiting.*

The clock ticks.

MARA. Look.

NAZIA *looks at the clock. It's gone nine.*

NAZIA. Shit. That's never happened before.

Pause.

MARA. Do you think something's wrong?

LEANNE *enters.*

LEANNE. Morning all. Both. Sorry I'm late.

She sits down.

Let's get started.

NAZIA. Where're Zoe and Mike?

LEANNE. They're not able to join us right now so I'm going to run the / meeting instead

NAZIA. Why? What's going on?

LEANNE. We're going to explain everything properly later but for now we just need to crack on. Okay? It's nine… oh-two, good morning and welcome to Morning Meeting.

NAZIA/MARA.…Good morning.

LEANNE (*brisk*). First up parish notices, Mara's got a key-nurse session with Mike at eleven fifteen, Nazia you're on leave from five so remember to sign out, and Suzanne will be coming off bed rest on Monday so she'll be joining us in meetings from next week.

There's a muffled shout from offstage. MARA *and* NAZIA *turn towards it.*

Helpful Thoughts please. Mara.

MARA. Er… yesterday I found my outpatient meeting helpful because it made me feel more relaxed about leaving.

LEANNE. Thank you. Yesterday I thought the way you two supported each other in a difficult group situation was very helpful.

NAZIA. Yesterday I found it helpful writing a –

There's another shout from offstage.

LEANNE. Yes?

NAZIA. Yesterday I found it helpful writing a letter to… I'm sorry, I can't concentrate.

LEANNE. I know it's tough but we do need to get / through this

NAZIA. Is she being put on bed rest?

MARA. Is she being sectioned?

LEANNE. We can't let the whole structure of the unit fall apart because of / one person

NAZIA. Can you stop treating us like kids and just tell us what's – !

ZOE enters. She makes a beeline for MARA.

ZOE. Are you happy now?

LEANNE. Bloody hell. Mike!

ZOE. After everything you put us through!

MIKE enters.

MIKE. Zoe, come on, come outside.

ZOE. Is this what you wanted? GET OFF ME.

MARA. What's she talking about?

LEANNE. Stop it now, you're making a scene.

ZOE. Oh am I? Am I making a FUCKING SCENE?

She kicks a chair across the room.

MARA. Jesus	NAZIA. What	LEANNE.	MIKE. ZOE!
Christ!	the fuck!	STOP!	

General chaos. LEANNE *gets in between* ZOE *and the other patients to de-escalate.*

LEANNE (*to* MIKE). Go and get her bag!

MIKE. I should stay, I can't –

LEANNE. I can handle her, go!

MIKE *leaves. Over this:*

ZOE. How come you didn't do this to her? When she was screaming, throwing shit, shit that *I* had clean up! How come she didn't get kicked out?!

MARA. What?   NAZIA. You're kicking her
                                                            out?

ZOE. Is it because she's younger? Because she's sectioned? Because she's thinner?

LEANNE. This isn't about Mara / or anyone else

ZOE. Of course it is, she fucking told you!

MARA. I don't know what you're talking about!

ZOE. Don't lie!

MARA. I didn't tell them anything!

NAZIA. It was me.

ZOE.…What?

NAZIA. I – I'm sorry, I didn't know they would do this, I thought I was helping you.

ZOE. *Helping* me?!

NAZIA. You were making it so difficult for everyone else and I thought they would help you to stop –

ZOE. Wow!   LEANNE. You did the right
                                                     thing Nazia.

NAZIA. You're the one who was going on about how important it is to be honest!

ZOE. You fucking hypocrite, what about when you were
    exercising in the toilet six times a day, I never told them
    about that!

NAZIA. Yeah well maybe you should have done!

LEANNE. Listen to me, this isn't happening because you were
    purging, it's because we gave you chance after chance to be
    honest with us and you just wouldn't do it Zoe. You know
    we can't keep you in here forever because you don't want to
    leave, if you're not willing to work with us –

ZOE. But I am willing, I'm willing! It was once, I made
    a mistake *once* –

LEANNE. We know it was more than once.

ZOE. But it's only been over the last week! When I said before
    that I hadn't been purging I was telling the truth and I wanted
    to tell you I did / and I'm sorry but

LEANNE. We've heard it all before.

ZOE. I'll work harder, I'll change, you can put me back on
    Constant, you can do whatever you want!

LEANNE. I'm sorry.

ZOE. What do you want from me? Do you want me to get on
    the floor and beg?

    MIKE *re-enters*.

MIKE. She's here.

LEANNE. I – already?

ZOE. What?

NAZIA. What?

LEANNE. I can tick off her inventory.

MIKE. I'll do it.

LEANNE. Okay but we need to be quick about it.

ZOE. Who's here?

NAZIA (*quiet, realising*). Oh, fuck.

LEANNE. Are you still going to do the –

MIKE. Yes.

ZOE. The what? / Do the what?

LEANNE. It'll have to be in here because the bedroom needs cleaning.

ZOE. Oh my god. You're admitting someone?!

LEANNE. I'll bring her in in five, yes?

ZOE. They must be fucking ill if you couldn't even wait three days till Mara left, who are they?

LEANNE. Mike, in five?

MIKE. Yes.

ZOE. WHO ARE THEY.

LEANNE. It doesn't matter who they are –

ZOE. Of course it matters, you're vacating my fucking bed to make room for them!

LEANNE. That's not what this is about, okay, it's a / separate situation

ZOE. Don't patronise me, you think I'm too stupid to understand how all this works? I'm not leaving.

MIKE. Please don't make this harder than it / needs to be

ZOE. I'm not leaving! Whoever it is they can sleep in the corridor because I'm not going.

LEANNE. You don't have a choice.

ZOE. What are you gonna do, get a reverse section? (*Re: Mara.*) Drag me out of the building like you dragged her in? What are you gonna do?

LEANNE. We'll have to call the police.

Beat.

ZOE. What?!

LEANNE. At that point you'd be trespassing on hospital
property –

ZOE. Oh my god! / (*To* MIKE.) Is she fucking serious?!

LEANNE. And nobody wants that to happen, believe me, but
you'd be leaving / us with no choice

ZOE. Mike… *Mike!*

MIKE. She's right.

ZOE. / Jesus Christ!

LEANNE. The best thing you can do is try to accept / the
situation

ZOE (*to* MIKE). I bet you're loving this aren't you? Getting to
sit in the office in the big-boy chair, in the doctors' ears
deciding who's worth saving and who's expendable –

MIKE. That's not what's / happening

ZOE. Does it satisfy something in you, bossing all these women
around? Are you projecting? An ex-girlfriend is it? Your
mother?

LEANNE. / Zoe, enough.

ZOE. Or is this how you keep a lid on your own impulses, is
this how you get your control?

LEANNE. I would think very carefully about what you're
saying / right now

ZOE. Am I right?

LEANNE. I understand that you're angry –

ZOE. You understand fuck-all!

LEANNE. But hurling abuse at us isn't going to change / the
situation

ZOE (*to* MIKE). You think you're so much better than her but
you're not, you're worse, you're supposed to understand!

LEANNE. Mike I really think I should / deal with this

ZOE (*to* MIKE). And you can't stand that I know that, can you?

LEANNE. Mike.

ZOE. I bet you're relieved to be rid of me, I bet you're fucking thrilled!

MIKE. Do you think I wanted this to happen?

ZOE. I didn't see you complaining when they were delivering the death sentence!

MIKE. I'm a key nurse Zoe, I'm not the one in charge, what do you want me to do?

ZOE. I want you to defend me, I want you to fucking *help* me, isn't that your *job*?!

MIKE (*snapping*). I TRIED. If they had it their way you would have left two weeks ago. I pushed for you to stay. So don't tell me I didn't try to help you, I did. You wouldn't let me.

Silence.

All at once the anger goes out of ZOE.

I'm sorry.

I'm sorry, I didn't mean that, I –

ZOE. Don't.

You're right.

Oh god, what have I done. What am I gonna do.

LEANNE *leaves.*

MIKE. Let me call Gemma.

ZOE. No.

MIKE. Let me call her and tell her you're leaving.

ZOE. Oh god no.

MIKE. I can ask her to pick you up at the station when you get home.

ZOE. I can't, please.

MIKE. You can't do this on your own.

ZOE. Please, please shut up.

MIKE. She wants to help.

ZOE. I don't deserve it.

MIKE. Yes you do, whatever's happened in the past she loves you and so does Molly.

ZOE. She doesn't, Molly hates me, she –

MIKE. She doesn't hate you, nobody hates you. Let me call Gemma.

ZOE. No, I can't, I can't face her, I can't face either of them, I can't look them in the eye ever again.

MIKE. They understand you weren't well –

ZOE. No, you don't know, you weren't there, you didn't see the look on her face when she saw what she saw, Christ, do you have any idea what it's like to have a *child* look at you like that, with such *pity*?

MIKE. That was your illness.

ZOE. Oh god I want to throw up. I need to throw up.

MIKE. Listen to me. What happened, the car, all of it, that was your illness.

ZOE. I am my illness.

MIKE. No you're not.

ZOE. Yes I am, it's been twenty-five years, there's no difference any more!

MIKE. There is a difference, there's a very big difference and this is what it wants Zoe, it wants you to be isolated –

ZOE. / Stop

MIKE. It wants you all to itself and I know right now that it's screaming in your ear –

ZOE. Stop / saying 'it'

MIKE. And telling you you're worthless and you're evil and if
    you just give in to it –

ZOE. / Stop it, stop saying 'it'

MIKE. Then it can make you feel better, but I'm telling you you
    don't have to listen to it and you can beat this.

ZOE. I can't.

MIKE. Yes you can.

ZOE. No I can't, I'm not like the others, I can't.

NAZIA. You can Zoe.

ZOE. You don't understand.

NAZIA. We do understand. We know how hard it is but you can
    do it.

MIKE. She's right.

ZOE. It's too late, it's too late.

MARA. It isn't Zoe, it's not too late.

ZOE. Yes it is! Yes it is!

NAZIA. Why?

ZOE. BECAUSE I HAVE NOTHING ELSE. I've got no future,
    I've got no life, I've got no job, I'll never have a family, I've
    got no friends, I have nothing, nothing left in me except this.
    I used to think there was an edge, I used to think there was
    an end / I used to think

MIKE. There can be an end / if you

ZOE. JUST LISTEN TO ME, I used to think there was this
    thing, in here, this awful rotting evil thing inside me and if
    I could just get small enough and deep enough and as close
    to the edge as possible, as close to the edge of living without
    actually dying I might be able to see it and reach in and rip it
    out but I've been there, I got there I saw the end and I came

back and I thought that would save me but it hasn't because it has sucked every cell out of my body and filled me up with itself and now it's just me, I am it and it is me and it'll never go away because without it I am nothing and so I *can't* give it up, no matter how much I want to I can't because when everyone leaves when everyone goes and everything goes I'll still have it and it's *me* and it's *mine*. And I hate it and it'll kill me but it's the only thing I know how to…

She buckles, exhausted. It's not big and shouty and dramatic. She just dissolves.

An incredibly public private grief.

MARA (*to* NAZIA, *gently*). Come on.

MARA leaves. NAZIA stays for a moment longer, then leaves.

MIKE stands watching ZOE, at a loss. Then he leaves too.

She's alone.

This should go on for long enough to make us think no one's ever coming back.

But then MIKE *returns with a scrap of paper.*

MIKE. This is her number. Take it.

He holds it out to her.

(*Putting it in her hand.*) Please.

LEANNE enters, holding a new folder and wheeling a suitcase.

SAM is behind her.

She looks awful.

The sight of her hits ZOE like a physical blow.

LEANNE. I'm sorry, we're gonna have to…

LEANNE goes over to ZOE's box, peels off the label and replaces it with a new one.

A terrible silence.

Then ZOE *picks up her bag, makes for the door. When she gets there, she stops. Without turning back:*

ZOE. Don't fuck it up this time.

Scene Five

Three days later.

It's the end of lunch; MARA *is stood giving her discharge speech. She's holding Sam's copy of Nietzsche.*

SAM *is wearing the same jumper that Leanne gave her in Act One.*

MARA. I'm not very good at this sort of thing. I've never really had a reason to do a speech before and whenever I tried to write it, I couldn't find the words to say what I wanted to say. But I read this thing the other day and it really made me think about my time here, and my life, and what I want from it, and what I don't want. So I thought I'd share that with you instead. I hope that's okay. It starts out kind of depressing but it gets good towards the end.

'What if, one day or night, some demon were to steal after you in your loneliest loneliness and say to you: "This life as you now live it and have lived it, you will have to live once more and innumerable times more. And there will be nothing new in it, but every pain and every joy and every thought and sigh and everything unspeakably small or great in your life will happen again, all in the same order and sequence – even this spider and this moonlight between the trees, and even this moment and I myself. The eternal hourglass of existence is turned upside down again and again, and you with it, speck of dust!"

'Would you not throw yourself down and gnash your teeth and curse the demon who said this? Or would you experience a tremendous moment when you would answer him: "You are a god and never have I heard anything more divine." If this thought took hold of you, it would transform you as you are, or perhaps crush you. The question in each and every thing: "Do you desire this once more and innumerable times more?" would lie upon your actions as the greatest weight. Or how well-disposed would you have to become to yourself and to life, to want nothing more than this?'

Thank you.

LEANNE *comes up to* MARA *with a tray of paint.* MARA *dips her hand into it and presses a handprint onto the mural of the tree.*

Everyone except SAM *claps.*

MARA *hugs* MIKE *and* LEANNE.

LEANNE. Congratulations. We're so proud of you.

MIKE. You've done so well.

MARA. Thank you. Thanks guys.

She hugs NAZIA.

Look after yourself, yeah?

NAZIA. Yeah. See you on the outside.

MARA. I'll hold you to that.

MARA *comes up to* SAM *and puts her book on the table.*

Bye Sam. Thanks, for.

SAM *stares at the book. Doesn't respond.*

LEANNE. Let's vamanos, shall we? Your brother's outside.

LEANNE *ushers* MARA *and* NAZIA *out. From the door:*

Mike. Five minutes.

MIKE. Yep.

LEANNE *exits.*

MIKE *places a glass of Ensure in front of* SAM.

He sits down opposite her.

SAM *has her hands in her lap, opening and closing her fingers around one wrist.*

Silence.

Can you put your hands on the table for me please?

Silence.

Why don't we start by just picking up the glass.

Silence.

Come on, Sam. I know it's tough but it's just what needs to happen.

Silence.

If we get this over with now, we can think of something nice to do this evening to take your mind off things.

Silence.

Do you want me to book you on the phone rota? So you can talk to your mum?

Silence.

Or we can play a board game? We just got some new ones.

Silence.

Look I understand if you're upset Leanne's not your key nurse again. I'm really sorry that's the way things worked out but –

SAM. I don't care about that.

Beat.

MIKE. Okay. Well you've barely said two words all week. It's going to be much harder for me to help if you don't try to talk to me.

Silence.

SAM *rubs at the bone in her wrist.*

What are you thinking?

Silence.

Maybe you're thinking this is a big step backwards? That this has all been a waste of time. I'd understand if you felt that way. But we can't change what's happened. All we can do now is think about how to move forwards. I want you to get well and get out of here so you can go back to university and / get on with

SAM. I'm not going back.

MIKE. Why?

SAM. They couldn't keep my place.

MIKE. Could you reapply?

Why don't we set that as an objective for this week. Why don't we look into that and see if –

SAM. There's no point. I'll just fuck it up again.

MIKE. That's not – you didn't fuck anything up.

SAM. Zoe thought so.

MIKE. Zoe wasn't talking to you.

Beat. SAM *picks at the table.*

SAM. It's my fault isn't it.

MIKE. What is?

SAM. That she got worse. That she's gone.

MIKE. No. None of this is your fault.

SAM. Will she be okay?

MIKE. I hope so.

SAM. Do you think so?

MIKE. I hope so. She won't be on her own. She'll have her outpatient team.

SAM. Will she come back?

Beat.

MIKE. I don't know. Maybe not here. Maybe somewhere else. But I don't know.

SAM *gets up, goes to the wall of handprints.*

SAM. What about Mara?

MIKE. Sam.

SAM. It was a nice speech. I never read that bit.

MIKE. Can you come and / sit down

SAM. I never even finished the book.

MIKE. Sam. Please.

SAM. Do you think she'll come back?

MIKE. What?

SAM. Do you think Mara will come back? Here.

MIKE. I hope not.

SAM. But you don't know.

MIKE. I don't think so. But you can never know for sure.

SAM. How many of these are identical? How many people end up coming back?

MIKE. Some. Not all.

SAM. Most?

MIKE. Whatever happens to other people isn't relevant. This is about you.

SAM. Did you think I'd come back?

Pause.

She tried to stop me. Zoe. Did she tell you that? I was awful to her. I do that. I say awful things. But she was right. I thought I was different because I had a reason to get better. Didn't matter in the end.

MIKE. You are different.

SAM. Why?

MIKE: Because you're a different person. And Zoe's been ill for a lot longer than you have.

SAM. So she's incurable.

MIKE. No. She's not incurable. Nobody's incurable.

SAM. But not everyone gets better do they.

I don't even know what that means any more.

Silence.

MIKE *looks at the Ensure. Looks at his watch.*

MIKE. Look, Sam –

SAM. I did try. I know you all think I didn't but I did.

MIKE. I don't think that.

SAM. Everyone else does. My mum does. But I really did try.

MIKE. I know you did, but we need to keep trying. You do know that under the terms of your section, if you don't manage to drink this we'll have to go upstairs so Leanne and I can help you. I know you don't want that to happen. I don't want that to happen. But we can't afford to carry on like this any longer.

Silence.

MIKE *looks at his watch again.*

The five minutes are up.

He goes to stand –

SAM. The last time we were together as a family was the day I got out of the children's unit.

MIKE *stills.*

My mum and dad took me to this Italian restaurant we used to go to every week when I was little. 'That's Amore', they called it, in the retail park. It was like a family tradition. They thought it would be nice. And they were so happy I was out, that things were 'normal' again. They bought a cake and everything. I mean they really thought...

Then the food came and I said, no. I'm not having it. I'm not hungry. I'll never forget the looks on their faces. Like I'd punched them. They started begging and pleading and crying, arguing all over again about whose fault it was and eventually my mum got so frustrated she just snapped and pointed at this family sat near us and said, you know what Sam, I would give anything to have a child like that. Someone happy and normal who can just enjoy food and enjoy life instead of this sad, empty thing you've turned out to be.

My first week in halls, a load of people on my corridor got together in the kitchen and ordered pizzas. All of them sat round laughing, drinking, having a good time. It was like looking at a different fucking species, how they could just... without thinking, without... and I wanted, *so badly*, to be in that room, to be one of them. So said to myself, fuck it, I'm just gonna fucking – do it. I'm just gonna join in. I'm gonna be just like everyone else. I had one slice and I felt so fucking guilty I locked myself in my room for the rest of the night. Crying. Panicking out of my mind. Eventually someone knocked. I made something up about a stomach ache. Kept that excuse going for a few weeks if anyone invited me out, until it became... obvious. Then they stopped asking. I was so sure that if I just went somewhere where no one knew me, where no one knew me *as this*, I could just *be*... something else. But this is what I am. And however much I try to be normal, and happy, and enjoy food and enjoy things and enjoy life, I can't. It won't let me. So what's the point in fighting.

MIKE. Because you don't know that it's aways gonna be that way. It might take a long time, it might take a few goes round, but eventually / it can

SAM. How would you know?

MIKE. Because I know.

SAM. But how?

MIKE. I've seen it happen.

SAM. You don't know what happens to people when they leave. You said so yourself.

MIKE. I know not everyone has to struggle with this for the rest of their lives.

SAM. No you don't. You only know that once they're gone, you can wash your hands of them. You have no idea what it's really like, you have no idea what goes on inside people's –

MIKE *chucks his folder aside. Rubs his eyes. Exhausted.*
SAM *is taken aback by this open show of frustration. She shrinks, self-conscious.*

I'm sorry.

MIKE. Don't. Don't say sorry.

A silence.

Will you sit down?

Please.

SAM *sits.* MIKE *collects himself.*

I've met a lot of people, over the years. And you're right. For some of them it never goes away. They spend their whole lives in and out of places like this and the system can't figure out how to help them. And the longer it goes on, the harder it gets. The more ingrained it becomes. Until you can't separate yourself from it any more. I've met people who've had terrible things happen to them, people in so much pain they don't know how to numb it any other way, people who've been in it so long they can't even remember how it started and knowing doesn't help them to stop. I've known people die from it. And the cruellest part is, that's what everyone remembers them for, once they're gone.

But I also know lot of people who've managed to turn it around. People like you who thought it was impossible but bit by bit, one thing at a time, they learned how to let it go. For good. Not to live a life where it's a constant battle, but to live an actual life. I know you don't trust us. You've probably got a good reason not to. But I'm asking you to please trust me on this. Because I mean it when I tell you that I know.

So there are two roads you can go down. You can give up. And you're pretty much guaranteed to either die, or spend the rest of your life outside of it, just existing. Both of those options are horrendous but at least you know where you're going, right? Or – you can keep trying. And things might get easier. And life might not be perfect, but at least you'll have one. And over time, and with help, it might get quieter. And quieter. Until one day it's a whisper instead of a scream. And eventually you're so distracted by the noise around you, you can't even hear it at all. But you'll never find out, unless you keep trying. That's all any of us can do.

SAM *stares at the glass of Ensure.*

A pause.

She puts one hand on the table.

She stares at the glass.

Stares.

She clenches her fist.

A moment, then –

Darkness.

End.

A Nick Hern Book

Some Demon first published in Great Britain in 2024 as a paperback original by Nick Hern Books Limited, The Glasshouse, 49a Goldhawk Road, London W12 8QP, in association with Papatango Theatre Company

Some Demon copyright © 2024 Laura Waldren

Laura Waldren has asserted her right to be identified as the author of this work

Cover photography by Michael Wharley; design by Rebecca Pitt

Designed and typeset by Nick Hern Books, London
Printed in the UK by Mimeo Ltd, Huntingdon, Cambridgeshire PE29 6XX

A CIP catalogue record for this book is available from the British Library

ISBN 978 1 83904 317 8

www.nickhernbooks.co.uk/environmental-policy

www.nickhernbooks.co.uk

facebook.com/nickhernbooks

twitter.com/nickhernbooks